THE TENNESSEE EXPLORER'S BUCKET LIST

Your Ultimate Travel Guide to Tennessee's Top Attractions

Brinn Palmer

Disclaimer:

The information provided in " **Tennessee Explorer's Bucket List: Your Ultimate Travel Guide to Tennessee 's Top Attractions**" is intended for general informational purposes only. While we strive to ensure the accuracy and reliability of the details within this guide, we cannot guarantee that all information is complete or up-to-date.

We strongly recommend that readers independently verify all details, including hours of operation, admission fees, transportation options, and the availability of attractions and accommodations before making any travel plans.

The inclusion of specific destinations, attractions, accommodations, or services in this guide does not imply endorsement or recommendation by the publisher. Travelers should exercise their own judgment and discretion when exploring and take necessary precautions for their safety and well-being.

The publisher disclaims any liability for any loss, injury, or inconvenience that may occur as a result of using the information presented in this guide. Travel with awareness, and enjoy discovering all that it has to offer.

All rights reserved. No part of this publication may be reproduced, distributed, or transmitted in any form or by any means, including photocopying, recording, or other electronic or mechanical methods, without the prior written permission of the publisher. Exceptions are made for brief quotations used in critical reviews.

Copyright © By Brinn Palmer, 2024.

How to Use This Guide

This guide is your companion to exploring top attractions and hidden gems. Here's how to make the most of it:
- **Browse by Destination:** Explore different regions with top attractions and activities listed for each area.
- **Plan Your Itinerary:** Use detailed descriptions and tips to create a personalized travel plan.
- **Check Practical Information:** Review key details like hours of operation, fees, and transportation options before heading out.
- **Personalize Your Adventure:** Adapt the recommendations to fit your travel style and pace.
- **Stay Updated:** Double-check details like event dates or seasonal changes for the latest information.

Instruction For Using The Interactive QR Code Map

1. Open a QR code scanner app on your smartphone.
2. Allow the app to access your device's camera.
3. Position the QR code within the camera's viewfinder.
4. Scan the QR code by holding your device steady until it's detected.
5. After scanning, you will be linked to Google Maps, directing you to the exact location associated with the QR code.

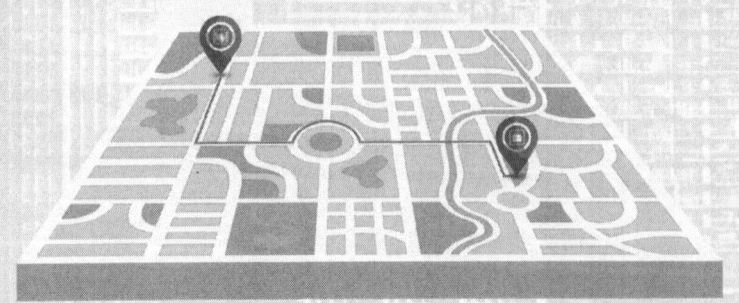

Table of Contents

Welcome to "Tennessee Explorer's Bucket List" 16
A Brief History of Tennessee 17
Why Choose Tennessee for Your Vacation? 21
Practical Information 23
    Getting to Tennessee 23
    Getting Around Tennessee 25
    Best Time to Visit Tennessee 26
    Food and Dining 27
    Local Etiquette and Customs 28
    Emergency Information and Safety Tips 28
Tennessee attractions 30
    Titanic Museum Attraction 30
    The Parthenon 31
    Andrew Jackson's Hermitage 32
    Bicentennial Capitol Mall State Park 33
    Nashville Zoo at Grassmere 34
    Honky Tonk Highway 36
    Dollywood 37
    Tennessee Aquarium 38
    Grand Ole Opry 40
    Centennial Park 41

Belle Meade Historic Site & Winery ... 42

Country Music Hall of Fame and Museum ... 43

Dolly's Tennessee Mountain Home ... 44

SOAR Adventure Tower ... 45

Nashville Shores ... 46

Walk of Fame Park ... 47

Nashville Public Square Park ... 48

Radnor Lake State Park ... 49

Madame Tussauds Nashville ... 50

Nashville WhatLiftsYou Wings Mural ... 51

Old Stone Fort State Archaeological Park ... 52

Cannonsburgh Village ... 53

Great Smoky Mountains National Park ... 54

2nd Avenue Historic District ... 55

Stones River National Battlefield ... 56

Carter House ... 57

Treetop Adventure Park at Nashville Shores ... 58

Cumberland Caverns ... 59

Rock Island State Park ... 60

The Chattanooga Zoo at Warner Park ... 61

Tennessee State Museum ... 62

Adventure Science Center ... 63

Cheekwood Estate & Gardens ... 64

The Escape Game Nashville (Downtown) ... 65

Escape Experience - Nashville Escape Games (Downtown) 66

Memory updated 67

Ryman Auditorium 68

Musicians Hall of Fame and Museum 69

Boro Beach 71

Charlie Daniels Park 72

Oaklands Mansion 73

Tennessee Tornado 74

Natchez Trace Parkway Bridge 76

Carnton 77

The Escape Game Nashville (Opry Mills) 78

Discovery Center at Murfree Spring 79

Lotz House Museum 80

Earth Experience - Middle Tennessee Museum of Natural History 81

Wander Nashville 82

The Cross 84

Shelby Bottoms Nature Center & Greenway 85

Tennessee Agricultural Museum 86

Tennessee Central Railway Museum 87

Fortress Rosecrans 88

Fred Deadman Park 89

Nelson's Green Brier Distillery 90

Patsy Cline Museum 91

NashTrash Tours 92

John Seigenthaler Pedestrian Bridge	93
Geographic Center of Tennessee	93
Steepest Pavement in Middle Tennessee	94
Parrot Mountain and Gardens	95
The Dolly Parton Experience	96
Historic Travellers Rest Historic House Museum	97
Downtown Lebanon	98
Pennington Cave	99
Nashville Looks Good On You Mural	100
Taylor Swift Bench	101
Rattle and Snap Plantation	102
Natchez Trace Parkway Sign	103
Rowing Man Statue	103
I Believe In Nashville Mural	104
Taylor Swift Willow Tree	105
Bigfoot Adventure TN Zipline	106
Historic Tours of Nashville	107
Shy's Hill	107
Buffalo Statues	108
What Lifts You - West Nashville Mural	109
Walter Hill Hydroelectric Station	110
Delta Riverboats	111
Old Town Trolley Tours Nashville	112

The Elephant Sanctuary in Tennessee – Elephant Discovery Center 113

"Musica" Statue 114

Belmont Mansion 115

Miller Gap Overlook 116

Hotels 117

Best Western Franklin Inn 117

Knights Inn Nashville 118

Hampton Inn McMinnville 119

Country Inn & Suites by Radisson, Nashville Airport East, TN 119

Best Western Heritage Inn 120

Wingate by Wyndham Goodlettsville 121

Super 8 by Wyndham Lakeland 122

Tennessee Mountain Lodge 123

Mountain Vista Inn & Suites 124

Red Roof Inn Knoxville Central - Papermill Road 125

Restaurants 126

Monell's 126

The Loveless Cafe 126

Skull's Rainbow Room 127

Log Cabin Restaurant 128

Darfons Restaurant + Bar 129

Feed Table and Tavern 129

The Row Kitchen & Pub 130

ix | Tennessee Explorer's Bucket List

Jeff Ruby's Steakhouse, Nashville 131

High Point Restaurant 132

The 404 Kitchen 132

Bell Buckle Cafe 133

Where to get souvenir 134

Nashville Gifts 134

Made in TN 135

Legends Gifts 135

The Nashville Store 136

Made in TN 137

Market Street Mercantile 137

Willie Nelson and Friends Museum and Nashville Souvenirs 138

The Opry Shop 139

Gift Horse 140

3-Day Itinerary 141

Day 1: Explore Nashville's Music History 141

Day 2: Pigeon Forge and Dollywood 142

Day 3: Discover the Great Smoky Mountains 143

7-Day Itinerary 145

Fun and Fascinating facts about Tennessee 152

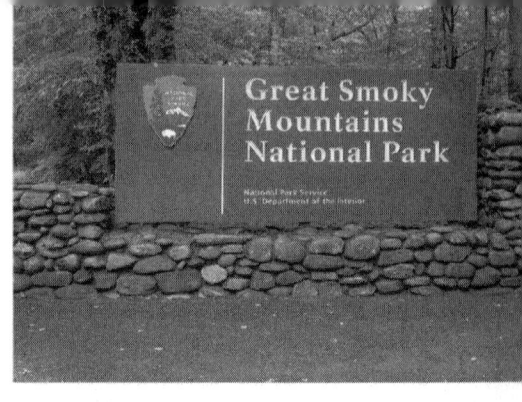

Welcome to " Tennessee Explorer's Bucket List"

Welcome to Tennessee, where adventure awaits around every corner. If this is your first time visiting Tennessee, get ready for an unforgettable journey through a state known for its rich culture, vibrant music, scenic landscapes, and deep-rooted history. Tennessee is a place where the rhythm of life moves to the sounds of country, blues, and rock 'n' roll, while the awe-inspiring beauty of its mountains, rivers, and valleys offers endless opportunities for adventure.

Our bucket list has been thoughtfully crafted to guide you through the best that Tennessee has to offer, whether you're visiting the bustling cities, exploring quaint small towns, or immersing yourself in the great outdoors. Here, you'll discover iconic landmarks like Graceland, the home of Elvis Presley, or stroll down the legendary Beale Street in Memphis, where live music fills the air every night. Dive into the heart of Nashville, the capital of country music, where you can visit the Grand Ole Opry, explore the Country Music Hall of Fame, or catch a live show at one of the many honky-tonks on Broadway.

But Tennessee isn't just about its cities. For nature lovers, the state is a treasure trove of outdoor adventures. The Great Smoky Mountains National Park, a UNESCO World Heritage site, offers breathtaking hikes, wildlife encounters, and sweeping mountain vistas. You can also take a scenic drive along the Natchez Trace Parkway or explore the crystal-clear waters of Norris Lake and the mighty Tennessee River.

History buffs will find plenty to explore as well. Tennessee played a significant role in shaping the nation's history, from Civil War battlefields like Shiloh and Stones River to the Tennessee State Museum, where you can learn about the state's impact on American culture and politics. The state is also home to several Civil Rights landmarks, including the National Civil Rights Museum in Memphis, housed in the Lorraine Motel where Dr. Martin Luther King Jr. was tragically assassinated.

Whether you're craving mouth-watering barbecue, local craft whiskey, or farm-to-table Southern cuisine, Tennessee's food scene is a journey in itself. Sample the legendary hot chicken of Nashville, the world-class barbecue in Memphis, or the fried catfish that's a staple across the state.

This bucket list will lead you to both the famous sights and the off-the-beaten-path treasures that only seasoned explorers discover. Whether you're catching a stunning sunset over the Cumberland Plateau, floating down the rivers of East Tennessee, or wandering through the state's countless festivals and fairs, there's always something new to experience. And while every visitor's journey is unique, one thing is certain—you'll leave Tennessee with memories to last a lifetime.

So pack your bags, embrace the spirit of exploration, and let the Tennessee adventure begin! Welcome to the Volunteer State, where music, history, nature, and southern hospitality await at every turn. Happy exploring!

A Brief History of Tennessee

Tennessee's history is deeply rooted in the cultural, social, and political landscape of the United States. Its journey from Native American lands to becoming a pivotal state in the Union is a story of expansion, conflict, resilience, and growth. Below is an exploration of the key moments and themes that define Tennessee's rich history.

Early Inhabitants: Native American History

Before European settlers arrived, Tennessee was home to various Native American tribes, most notably the Cherokee and Chickasaw. Archaeological evidence suggests that Native American presence in the region dates back over 12,000 years. These tribes thrived in Tennessee's fertile lands, forming complex societies with trade networks and agricultural systems.

The Cherokee, in particular, played a dominant role in the southeastern United States, controlling large swaths of land and establishing towns throughout the Tennessee River Valley. They were known for their sophisticated political systems and cultural contributions, including the creation of the Cherokee syllabary by Sequoyah in the 1820s.

European Exploration and Settlement

European exploration of Tennessee began in the mid-16th century when Spanish explorers like Hernando de Soto ventured into the region in search of riches. However, it wasn't until the late 17th century that French and English settlers began establishing trading posts along the Mississippi and Tennessee rivers.

The first permanent European settlers arrived in the mid-1700s, mostly of Scottish and Irish descent. They were drawn to the region by the abundant natural resources and fertile land. These settlers formed the Watauga Association in 1772, one of the first self-governing bodies in the American colonies, signifying Tennessee's early push for autonomy and self-determination.

The Formation of the State of Tennessee

The road to Tennessee's statehood was marked by political tensions and shifting allegiances. During the American Revolutionary War, many settlers in the region supported the patriot cause, hoping for independence from British rule and control over Native American lands. After the war, the region was part of North Carolina, but settlers increasingly felt neglected by the distant state government.

In 1784, settlers in the eastern part of Tennessee declared independence from North Carolina and formed the short-lived State of Franklin. Though the attempt to create a separate state failed, it highlighted the region's desire for self-governance.

In 1796, after petitioning the U.S. Congress, Tennessee was officially admitted as the 16th state of the Union. It was the first state to enter the Union after the original 13 colonies, and it was a moment of pride and celebration for the settlers who had fought for years to achieve this status.

Tennessee and the Trail of Tears

One of the most tragic chapters in Tennessee's history is its role in the Trail of Tears. In the 1830s, under President Andrew Jackson's Indian Removal Act, the U.S. government forcibly removed thousands of Cherokee people from their ancestral lands in Tennessee, Georgia, and North Carolina. The Cherokee were marched to present-day Oklahoma in a grueling journey that resulted in the deaths of thousands due to disease, starvation, and exhaustion.

Though Jackson, who was from Tennessee, saw the removal as a necessary step for American expansion, the Trail of Tears remains a dark legacy in both Tennessee's and America's history. Today, various sites in Tennessee, including the Cherokee Removal Memorial Park, commemorate the events and the suffering of the Cherokee people.

The Civil War and Tennessee's Role

Tennessee played a crucial role in the American Civil War, becoming a major battleground between Union and Confederate forces. In 1861, Tennessee was the last state to secede from the Union, but it was also the first state to be readmitted after the war.

Tennessee's geography made it strategically important, as major rivers like the Mississippi and Tennessee Rivers provided key transportation routes for both armies. The state was home to several significant battles, including the Battle of Shiloh, the Siege of Fort Donelson, and the Battle of Chattanooga.

Notably, Tennessee had divided loyalties during the war. While the state as a whole supported the Confederacy, the eastern part of Tennessee remained staunchly pro-Union. This division resulted in internal conflict within the state, as families and communities were torn apart by the war.

After the Civil War, Tennessee faced the difficult process of Reconstruction, as it worked to rebuild its economy and infrastructure. The abolition of slavery brought freedom to thousands of African Americans in Tennessee, but the state, like many others, struggled with issues of racial inequality and violence during the Reconstruction era.

The Civil Rights Movement

Tennessee was a key battleground during the Civil Rights Movement of the 1950s and 1960s. Memphis, in particular, played a central role, as it was the site of major protests and activism. African Americans in Tennessee fought for their rights through sit-ins, boycotts, and legal challenges to segregation.

One of the most significant events in Tennessee's civil rights history was the assassination of Dr. Martin Luther King Jr. in Memphis on April 4, 1968. King was in the city to support a sanitation workers' strike when he was shot on the balcony of the Lorraine Motel. His death was a devastating blow to the Civil Rights Movement, but it also galvanized efforts to continue the struggle for equality.

Today, the National Civil Rights Museum in Memphis, located at the Lorraine Motel, stands as a powerful tribute to Dr. King and the countless others who fought for civil rights in Tennessee and across the country.

Tennessee in the 20th Century: Economic Growth and Cultural Influence

Throughout the 20th century, Tennessee grew into a hub of economic activity and cultural influence. The state became known for its contributions to the music industry, particularly in the cities of Nashville and Memphis.

- **Nashville:** Often referred to as the "Country Music Capital of the World," Nashville became the epicenter of the country music industry, with iconic venues like the Grand Ole Opry and the rise of stars such as Hank Williams, Dolly Parton, and Johnny Cash.
- **Memphis:** Known for its contributions to blues, soul, and rock 'n' roll, Memphis produced legendary artists like Elvis Presley, B.B. King, and Otis Redding.

Economically, Tennessee shifted from an agrarian economy to a more diverse industrial economy in the mid-20th century. Manufacturing, automotive, and healthcare industries began to play a larger role, contributing to the state's overall growth.

Modern-Day Tennessee: A Cultural and Economic Powerhouse

In recent decades, Tennessee has continued to thrive, balancing its rich historical roots with modern development. Nashville's booming music and healthcare industries have made it one of the fastest-growing cities in the country, while Memphis remains a hub for logistics and transportation, with FedEx headquartered in the city.

Tourism is a major part of the state's economy, as millions of visitors flock to Tennessee each year to experience its music heritage, natural beauty, and historical landmarks. The Great Smoky Mountains National Park is the most visited national park in the United States, and sites like Graceland, Dollywood, and the Country Music Hall of Fame draw countless visitors.

Tennessee has also made significant strides in education and healthcare, with leading institutions such as Vanderbilt University and St. Jude Children's Research Hospital.

Why Choose Tennessee for Your Vacation?

Tennessee is an exceptional vacation destination, offering a diverse mix of attractions, natural beauty, and cultural experiences that cater to a wide range of interests. Whether you're an outdoor enthusiast, a music lover, or a history buff, here are some top reasons why Tennessee should be at the top of your travel list:

The Birthplace of American Music

Tennessee is widely regarded as the heart of American music. It's the birthplace of country, blues, rock 'n' roll, and soul music, offering unique experiences in cities like:

- **Nashville:** Known as "Music City," Nashville is home to the Grand Ole Opry, Country Music Hall of Fame, and countless live music venues.
- **Memphis:** The home of Elvis Presley and Beale Street, Memphis is where you'll find Sun Studio, Stax Museum, and Graceland, celebrating the King of Rock 'n' Roll.

Stunning Natural Landscapes

Tennessee is home to some of the most scenic natural landscapes in the country, making it ideal for outdoor adventures:

- **Great Smoky Mountains National Park:** America's most visited national park offers breathtaking views, hiking trails, waterfalls, and diverse wildlife.
- **Cumberland Plateau:** Known for its rugged terrain, this area is perfect for hiking, rock climbing, and exploring caves.
- **Rivers and Lakes:** Tennessee's vast network of rivers and lakes, including the Tennessee River and Douglas Lake, is perfect for boating, fishing, and water sports.

Rich History and Heritage

Tennessee played a crucial role in U.S. history, from the Civil War to the Civil Rights Movement:

- **Civil War Sites:** Explore battlegrounds like Shiloh National Military Park or visit historical homes that survived the war.

- **Civil Rights Landmarks:** Learn about the fight for civil rights at the National Civil Rights Museum in Memphis, located at the Lorraine Motel where Dr. Martin Luther King Jr. was assassinated.
- **Pioneering History:** Visit sites like Davy Crockett's birthplace and the Museum of Appalachia to experience Tennessee's frontier spirit.

Southern Hospitality and Cuisine

Tennessee's famous Southern hospitality makes visitors feel welcome wherever they go. The state's culinary offerings are just as warm and inviting:

- **Memphis Barbecue:** World-renowned for its smoked meats and dry rubs, Memphis barbecue is a must-try for food lovers.
- **Southern Comfort Food:** Savor comfort dishes like fried chicken, biscuits and gravy, and pecan pie in charming local diners.
- **Whiskey Distilleries:** Tour iconic distilleries like Jack Daniel's in Lynchburg to learn about the state's whiskey-making traditions.

Affordable Travel Destination

Tennessee is an affordable vacation spot, offering great value for travelers. From budget-friendly hotels to free attractions like national parks and historical sites, visitors can enjoy a rich travel experience without breaking the bank.

Family-Friendly Attractions

Whether you're traveling with kids or just looking for wholesome fun, Tennessee has plenty of family-friendly destinations:

- **Dollywood:** This popular theme park in Pigeon Forge, owned by country music legend Dolly Parton, features thrilling rides, live entertainment, and seasonal festivals.
- **Tennessee Aquarium:** Located in Chattanooga, this top-rated aquarium offers fascinating exhibits and educational programs for visitors of all ages.
- **The Lost Sea Adventure:** Take a boat ride on America's largest underground lake in Sweetwater, a fun and educational experience for the whole family.

Festivals and Events Year-Round

Tennessee hosts a wide variety of festivals and events throughout the year, celebrating everything from music and culture to food and art:

- **Bonnaroo Music and Arts Festival:** One of the nation's largest music festivals, held annually in Manchester, TN.
- **Memphis in May:** A month-long festival featuring music, food, and cultural events, including the world-famous World Championship Barbecue Cooking Contest.
- **Tennessee State Fair:** Experience local culture, agriculture, and family fun at this beloved event held every fall.

Practical Information

Welcome to Tennessee! Whether you're planning a short visit or an extended stay, knowing practical details about your destination is essential for a smooth and enjoyable experience. Tennessee offers a wealth of experiences, from vibrant cities to serene countryside, but there are important things to consider before you embark on your journey. In this guide, we'll cover everything from transportation options and weather patterns to safety tips and local customs, helping you navigate Tennessee like a seasoned traveler.

Getting to Tennessee

Tennessee is centrally located in the southeastern United States, making it easily accessible by air, road, and rail.

By Air

Tennessee is home to several major airports:

- **Nashville International Airport (BNA):** Located in Nashville, the state's busiest airport serves numerous domestic and international flights.
- **Memphis International Airport (MEM):** Known for its large cargo traffic (FedEx's global hub is here), this airport also provides a variety of passenger flights.

- **McGhee Tyson Airport (TYS):** Located near Knoxville, it offers convenient access to the Great Smoky Mountains and eastern Tennessee.
- **Chattanooga Metropolitan Airport (CHA):** This smaller airport offers regional flights, especially for visitors headed to Chattanooga and its surrounding attractions.

Most visitors choose to fly into Nashville or Memphis, given their extensive flight options, and then travel by road to other parts of the state.

By Car

Tennessee is intersected by several major interstate highways, making road travel simple:
- **I-40:** Runs east to west across the entire state, connecting Memphis, Nashville, and Knoxville.
- **I-65:** Runs north to south through Nashville, connecting with Kentucky to the north and Alabama to the south.
- **I-75:** Travels from Chattanooga in the south through Knoxville and heads northeast toward Virginia and Kentucky.
- **I-24:** Links Nashville to Chattanooga in the southeast.

These well-maintained highways offer convenient access to key destinations, whether you're exploring the cities or venturing into Tennessee's natural landscapes.

By Bus

Bus services such as **Greyhound** and **Megabus** connect Tennessee's major cities with other parts of the U.S. These options are budget-friendly but can be slower than other modes of travel.

By Train

Amtrak offers a rail service into Memphis via its **City of New Orleans** route, which runs between Chicago and New Orleans. Train travel may not be as widespread as other options, but it can be a scenic and comfortable way to arrive in western Tennessee.

Getting Around Tennessee

Once you've arrived in Tennessee, getting around is easy, though options vary depending on the region.

Driving

Renting a car is often the most convenient way to explore Tennessee, especially if you're visiting multiple cities or heading into rural areas. All major car rental companies operate in Tennessee's airports and cities, offering a range of vehicles from compact cars to SUVs.

- **Driving laws:** Tennessee drives on the right-hand side of the road, and seatbelts are mandatory for all passengers. The legal speed limit is typically 70 mph (113 km/h) on highways, 55 mph (88 km/h) on rural roads, and 30 mph (48 km/h) in urban areas unless otherwise posted.
- **Parking:** Parking is generally easy to find in Tennessee's smaller towns, but urban areas like Nashville and Memphis can be more challenging. Most cities have metered parking, garages, and public lots. Be aware of parking restrictions and always check for signs indicating where parking is prohibited.

Public Transportation

In the larger cities, public transportation systems are available, but services vary in coverage and convenience.

- **Nashville:** The **WeGo Public Transit** system offers bus routes throughout the city and a few surrounding areas. Additionally, the **Music City Star** is a commuter rail service running between downtown Nashville and the eastern suburbs.
- **Memphis:** The **Memphis Area Transit Authority (MATA)** operates buses, trolley cars in downtown Memphis, and a limited paratransit service.
- **Knoxville:** The **Knoxville Area Transit (KAT)** system provides bus services with routes across the city and university areas.

While public transportation can be useful in urban areas, those traveling beyond the cities will find it limited. Renting a car or using rideshare services like **Uber** and **Lyft** is often more practical for getting around outside major metro areas.

Cycling

Cycling is becoming more popular in Tennessee, especially in Nashville, Knoxville, and Chattanooga, where you'll find dedicated bike lanes and bike-share programs like **BCycle**. Many of Tennessee's state parks and national parks, like the Great Smoky Mountains, also have excellent cycling trails for recreational riding.

Best Time to Visit Tennessee

Tennessee's climate is generally mild and pleasant, but it does vary across the state, with more distinct seasonal changes in the mountainous eastern regions.

Spring (March to May)

Spring is one of the best times to visit Tennessee. Temperatures range from 50°F to 70°F (10°C to 21°C), making it ideal for outdoor activities like hiking, visiting parks, or exploring cities. Springtime also brings beautiful blooms, particularly in the Great Smoky Mountains, which are home to wildflower hikes and other scenic views.

Summer (June to August)

Summer in Tennessee can be hot and humid, with temperatures ranging from 70°F to 90°F (21°C to 32°C). If you plan to visit during the summer, prepare for higher humidity, especially in western and central Tennessee. Despite the heat, summer is peak season for music festivals, outdoor events, and water-based activities such as boating and swimming at Tennessee's many lakes and rivers.

Fall (September to November)

Fall is another popular time to visit, especially in the eastern parts of the state, where the autumn foliage is stunning. Temperatures cool down to between 55°F and 75°F (13°C to 24°C), providing perfect conditions for outdoor adventures. Harvest festivals and fall events take place statewide, and the Great Smoky Mountains become a vibrant display of red, orange, and yellow leaves.

Winter (December to February)
Winters in Tennessee are relatively mild, particularly in the lower elevations, with temperatures ranging from 30°F to 50°F (-1°C to 10°C). Snowfall is rare in cities like Nashville and Memphis but more common in the Smoky Mountains. Winter is a good time for exploring indoor attractions like museums or enjoying a cozy cabin stay in the mountains.

Food and Dining

Tennessee's food scene is a highlight for many visitors, offering everything from traditional Southern comfort food to innovative modern cuisine. Whether you're sampling Nashville's famous hot chicken or Memphis' legendary barbecue, there's something to satisfy every palate.

Nashville Hot Chicken
A spicy fried chicken dish that originated in Nashville, hot chicken is a must-try for anyone visiting the city. Head to **Prince's Hot Chicken Shack** or **Hattie B's** for an authentic experience, but be prepared for some serious heat!

Memphis Barbecue
Memphis is one of the BBQ capitals of the U.S., known for its slow-cooked, dry-rubbed pork ribs and pulled pork sandwiches. Some of the most famous spots include **Central BBQ**, **Gus's World Famous Fried Chicken**, and the iconic **Rendezvous** in downtown Memphis.

Southern Comfort Food
In Tennessee, you'll find plenty of Southern classics like biscuits and gravy, fried catfish, collard greens, and cornbread. Visit local diners and family-owned restaurants to experience homemade, down-home cooking. Some favorites include **Loveless Café** near Nashville and **Arnold's Country Kitchen** for a classic meat-and-three meal.

Farm-to-Table Movement
In recent years, Tennessee has embraced the farm-to-table movement, with many restaurants sourcing fresh, local ingredients. Cities like

Chattanooga, Knoxville, and Nashville are home to a growing number of chefs focused on sustainable, organic, and locally-grown produce.

Local Etiquette and Customs

Tennessee is known for its Southern hospitality, and visitors are often struck by the friendliness of the locals. However, it's helpful to be aware of a few cultural norms and customs to ensure a smooth and respectful visit.

General Politeness

Tennesseans value politeness and courtesy. Simple gestures like saying "please," "thank you," and "excuse me" go a long way in everyday interactions. People tend to be friendly, and you may find that strangers will engage you in conversation or offer help if needed.

Addressing People

It's common to address people, especially older individuals, as "sir" or "ma'am" out of respect. If you're unsure how to address someone, it's better to err on the side of formality.

Tipping

Tipping is expected at restaurants, with the standard being 15% to 20% of the total bill. You should also tip service workers such as taxi drivers, hotel staff, and bartenders. For exceptional service, a higher tip is appreciated.

Emergency Information and Safety Tips

While Tennessee is generally a safe place to visit, it's always important to stay aware of your surroundings and take precautions. Here's what you need to know about safety and emergencies during your trip.

Emergency Numbers

- **911:** This is the standard emergency number for police, fire, and medical emergencies.

Safety Tips
- **In Cities:** Keep your belongings secure, especially in crowded areas or tourist hotspots. Be cautious at night, particularly in less-populated areas, and use rideshare services if needed.
- **Outdoor Safety:** If you're hiking or spending time in Tennessee's national parks, always follow posted signs and stay on marked trails. Bring plenty of water and be aware of wildlife, especially in rural or mountainous areas.

Natural Disasters

Tennessee is prone to a few natural hazards, particularly tornadoes and severe thunderstorms. During spring and summer, storms can pop up quickly, so it's important to monitor local weather reports. Tornado warnings should be taken seriously, and visitors should familiarize themselves with the safety protocols at their accommodations.

Tennessee Attractions

Titanic Museum Attraction

Location: 2134 Parkway, Pigeon Forge, TN 37863, United States
Plus Code: RCCC+6C Pigeon Forge, Tennessee, USA
Website: www.titanicpigeonforge.com
Contact: +1 417-334-9500
Opening Hours:
- Monday to Sunday: 9am – 8pm

Description: The Titanic Museum Attraction in Pigeon Forge is a detailed, immersive experience designed to resemble the iconic ship. Visitors are immediately drawn in by the exterior, which is a half-scale replica of the Titanic itself. Inside, the museum showcases a vast collection of authentic artifacts, personal stories of the passengers, and a historical timeline of the ship's ill-fated voyage. One of the main features is its interactive exhibits where visitors can touch an iceberg and attempt to walk on sloping decks that simulate the ship's conditions during its sinking. These elements add a tactile layer to the educational journey, making it suitable for families and individuals interested in history. The museum is self-guided, with audio tours available, though some visitors report issues with the device, so patience may be required. Guests should plan for a wait time of 10-30 minutes, and it is highly recommended to make a reservation in advance, especially during weekends when the museum can be crowded. Tickets are reasonably priced considering the depth of the experience, with a well-stocked gift shop offering affordable Titanic-themed souvenirs.

Admission: Prices are available on the official website, www.titanicpigeonforge.com, and vary depending on age and group size, typically ranging from $30 to $40 USD.

Nearby Attractions: The museum is located near other popular Pigeon Forge attractions such as Dollywood, The Island in Pigeon Forge, and the Smoky Mountain Alpine Coaster.

Important Information for Visitors: While the museum is designed for visitors of all ages, it may be less engaging for very young children. Reservations are strongly recommended to avoid long wait times. Visitors are encouraged to arrive early to fully enjoy the exhibits at a relaxed pace.

The Parthenon

Location: 2500 West End Ave, Nashville, TN 37203, United States
Plus Code: 45XP+VM Nashville, Tennessee, USA
Website: www.nashvilleparthenon.com
Contact: +1 615-862-8431
Opening Hours:
- Monday to Thursday: 9am – 7pm
- Friday to Saturday: 9am – 4:30pm
- Sunday: 12:30pm – 4:30pm

Description: The Parthenon in Nashville is a full-scale replica of the original Parthenon in Athens, Greece. Situated in the heart of Centennial Park, this iconic structure serves as both a museum and a monument to ancient Greek culture. Visitors are greeted by the massive gilded statue of Athena, a stunning recreation of the goddess that was central to the ancient temple. The museum within the Parthenon offers an extensive collection of art and historical exhibits that highlight the cultural and architectural significance of the original structure. There are also educational areas for children, making it a family-friendly destination.

The surrounding grounds of Centennial Park are well-maintained and offer plenty of recreational space where visitors can enjoy picnics, feed ducks, or simply relax. The park is a popular spot for locals and tourists alike, with various activities such as yoga, soccer, and walking tours. For those who wish to learn more about the history, there is a self-guided walking tour accessible via QR codes located around the area.

Admission: Ticket prices range from $6 to $10 USD depending on age, and tickets can be purchased on-site.

Nearby Attractions: The Parthenon is located within Centennial Park, a large public park in Nashville that also hosts seasonal events, festivals, and outdoor performances. Other nearby attractions include the Vanderbilt University campus and the nearby West End shopping district.

Important Information for Visitors: While the museum inside The Parthenon is open to the public, Centennial Park remains accessible even when the building is closed. It is recommended to visit early in the day to avoid crowds, especially during weekends and public holidays. No reservation is required for entry.

Andrew Jackson's Hermitage

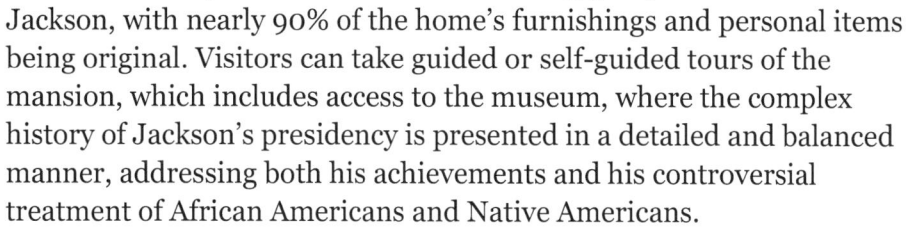

Location: 4580 Rachels Ln, Hermitage, TN 37076, United States
Plus Code: 697M+GV Hermitage, Nashville, TN, USA
Website: www.thehermitage.com
Contact: +1 615-889-2941
Opening Hours:
- Monday to Sunday: 9am – 5pm

Description: Andrew Jackson's Hermitage is the former home of the 7th U.S. President, Andrew Jackson, and a well-preserved historical landmark. The 1,120-acre plantation offers a fascinating glimpse into the life of Jackson, with nearly 90% of the home's furnishings and personal items being original. Visitors can take guided or self-guided tours of the mansion, which includes access to the museum, where the complex history of Jackson's presidency is presented in a detailed and balanced manner, addressing both his achievements and his controversial treatment of African Americans and Native Americans.

The estate also features beautiful, expansive gardens that serve as a peaceful counterpoint to the historical tours. The grounds include a family cemetery where Jackson and his wife are buried, and visitors can also take a horse-drawn wagon tour to explore the plantation further. The museum offers artifacts from Jackson's life and the period, along with interactive exhibits. While no photography is allowed inside the mansion, the surrounding property provides ample opportunities for

photos. A gift shop and café are available on-site, offering souvenirs and refreshments.
Admission: Tickets range from $15 to $25 USD, depending on the tour option chosen, and can be purchased at www.thehermitage.com.
Nearby Attractions: The Hermitage is located near the Stones River Greenway, a scenic walking trail, and the Nashville Shores Lakeside Resort.
Important Information for Visitors: Reservations are recommended for guided tours, especially on weekends and holidays. Visitors should note that while the museum provides an in-depth exploration of Andrew Jackson's legacy, some aspects of the tour may not be suitable for very young children due to the heavy historical content.

Bicentennial Capitol Mall State Park

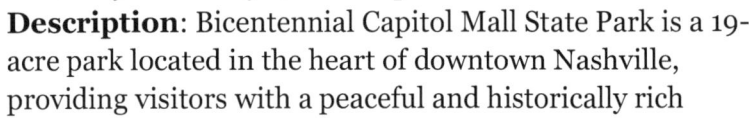

Location: 600 James Robertson Pkwy, Nashville, TN 37243, United States
Plus Code: 56C6+9X Nashville, Tennessee, USA
Website: www.tnstateparks.com
Contact: +1 888-867-2757
Opening Hours:
• Monday to Sunday: 7am – 10pm
Description: Bicentennial Capitol Mall State Park is a 19-acre park located in the heart of downtown Nashville, providing visitors with a peaceful and historically rich experience. Designed to commemorate Tennessee's 200th anniversary, this park offers wide open spaces for walking, resting, and exploring. The park features a variety of historical markers, including a 200-foot granite map of Tennessee, a World War II Memorial, and the striking Tennessee State Capitol Building in view from several vantage points. The Tennessee Rivers Fountain, which represents the state's major waterways, is a refreshing focal point of the park.
Visitors can walk along the Path of History, which details important moments in Tennessee's development, or sit in the outdoor

amphitheater with views of the Capitol. The park also hosts a globe monument that rotates on water, providing a unique and engaging visual experience. Restrooms are available on-site, located near the entrance and adjacent to the nearby Nashville Farmers' Market, which provides additional conveniences such as shopping and dining options. The park is dog-friendly and offers plenty of shaded areas, benches, and picnic spots, making it a perfect place to relax, enjoy nature, or learn about Tennessee's history.

Admission: Free

Nearby Attractions: The park is adjacent to the Nashville Farmers' Market, where visitors can explore local food vendors and shops. It is also within walking distance of the Tennessee State Capitol and the Tennessee State Museum, both offering additional historical insights.

Important Information for Visitors: The park is an excellent spot for families and those interested in history, with plenty of walking paths and shaded seating areas. Visitors should be aware that the park can become busy during weekends or special events, but it offers enough space to accommodate many visitors. Restrooms are well-maintained, and the park is accessible for visitors of all ages.

Nashville Zoo at Grassmere

Location: 3777 Nolensville Pk, Nashville, TN 37211, United States
Plus Code: 37Q5+Q2 Nashville, Tennessee, USA
Website: www.nashvillezoo.org
Contact: +1 615-833-1534
Opening Hours:
- Monday to Sunday: 9am – 6pm

Description: The Nashville Zoo at Grassmere is a popular family destination offering visitors the chance to see a diverse range of animals from around the world in a beautiful and well-maintained environment. Spread across 188 acres, the zoo is home to over 2,700 animals from 365 species, including tigers, kangaroos, and birds. The zoo is designed with plenty of tree cover, offering relief on hot days, and is complemented by air-conditioned indoor exhibits such as the aviary, aquarium, and vivarium, which provide a break from the outdoor areas. A must-see is the kangaroo enclosure, where visitors can get up close to the animals in a unique interactive experience.

Children can enjoy the zoo's highly rated playground, which offers a safe and fun space to play. Throughout the zoo, snack stands and restrooms are conveniently located, making it an easy and comfortable visit for families. Visitors have praised the knowledgeable and caring staff, who provide great insights into the animals and their care. While the food and drinks sold on-site can be expensive, the zoo allows visitors to bring their own, offering flexibility during the visit. The zoo also offers memberships for frequent visitors, making it an affordable option for locals.

Admission:
- Adults (13-64): $25
- Children (2-12): $18
- Seniors (65+): $22
- Members: Free

Nearby Attractions: The zoo is located near the historic Grassmere home, where visitors can explore the surrounding gardens and additional exhibits.

Important Information for Visitors: The zoo is best visited early in the day, especially on hot days, as many animals are more active in the morning. Be sure to take advantage of the shaded areas and indoor exhibits. Though reservations are recommended, especially on weekends, they are not always required, and wait times may vary depending on visitor traffic.

Honky Tonk Highway

Location: 501 Broadway, Nashville, TN 37203, United States
Plus Code: 566C+5J Nashville, Tennessee, USA
Website: www.visitmusiccity.com
Contact: +1 800-657-6910
Opening Hours:
- Monday to Sunday: 10am – 3am

Description: Honky Tonk Highway is an electrifying stretch of Broadway in downtown Nashville, renowned for its vibrant live music scene. This iconic strip is lined with numerous honky tonk bars where live performances fill the air every day, from early morning to the late hours of the night. You'll find a range of musical genres being played, from classic country to rock, modern pop, and more, making it a haven for music lovers. Each bar offers a unique atmosphere, many with multiple floors and rooftop views of the bustling streets below. The venues along Honky Tonk Highway do not charge cover fees, allowing visitors to freely explore the different bars, experience various live acts, and enjoy the dynamic energy that Nashville is famous for.

The area comes alive in the evening, with neon lights, energetic crowds, and an unmistakable vibe that invites everyone to dance, sing, and fully embrace the heart of Music City. It's a favorite spot for both locals and tourists, creating a friendly, welcoming environment where people from all walks of life can connect over their shared love for live music. While parking may be challenging, nearby garages and lots make access convenient. Visitors can feel safe with visible law enforcement ensuring a secure atmosphere. Honky Tonk Highway is a must-visit for anyone looking to experience Nashville's rich musical culture in a lively and unforgettable setting.

Dollywood

Location: 2700 Dollywood Parks Blvd, Pigeon Forge, TN 37863, United States
Plus Code: QFW9+2G Pigeon Forge, Tennessee, USA
Website: www.dollywood.com
Contact: +1 800-365-5996
Opening Hours:
Monday to Sunday: 10 am – 8 pm (hours may vary by season)
Admission (Ticket):
Adults: $89 USD
Children (ages 4–9): $79 USD
Seniors (60+): $79 USD

Season Passes are available
Description: Dollywood is a popular theme park located in the scenic Smoky Mountains of Tennessee, offering a blend of thrilling rides, musical entertainment, and traditional crafts. A full day is recommended to fully explore the park, as it features a variety of attractions, including roller coasters like the Wild Eagle, Mystery Mine, Tennessee Tornado, and the family-friendly Blazing Fury. For a slower-paced experience, the Dollywood Express steam train offers scenic rides through the park, particularly memorable after dusk.

Parking costs $25, and trams provide convenient transportation to the entrance. For a more convenient option, VIP parking is available for $50, allowing for easier access. Cool-down areas and shaded seating are available throughout the park, providing relief on hot days. Water is free, while sodas cost around $4, and souvenir cups are available for purchase. Visitors are encouraged to download the interactive map to help navigate the large park.

Dining at Dollywood can be expensive, with meals such as chicken tenders and fries costing $33. Many guests recommend bringing snacks or choosing more affordable options outside the park. The cinnamon bread from the park's bakery is highly recommended. Military discounts are offered, and it's highly advised to buy tickets online in advance to avoid long queues at the ticket counters.

Dollywood provides rides and entertainment for all ages, with plenty of live music and seasonal festivals throughout the year. For those visiting with children, there are play areas and milder attractions that cater to younger visitors. The park is also known for its friendly staff and clean, well-maintained grounds, ensuring an enjoyable experience for all.

Nearby Attractions:
- The Great Smoky Mountains National Park
- Patriot Park, offering trolley rides to Dollywood

Important Information for Visitors:
Parking costs $25, but a trolley from nearby Patriot Park is available for $3 per person, offering a cost-effective alternative. It's recommended to arrive early to avoid long lines, and purchasing tickets online is suggested. Dollywood is closed one day a week, so checking the park's schedule in advance is important.

Tennessee Aquarium

Location: 1 Broad St, Chattanooga, TN 37402, United States
Plus Code: 3M4Q+8H Chattanooga, Tennessee, USA
Website: www.tnaqua.org
Contact: +1 423-265-0695
Opening Hours:
Thursday: 10 am – 2 pm
Friday to Sunday: 10 am – 5 pm
Monday to Wednesday: 10 am – 5 pm
Admission (Ticket):
Adults: $34.95 USD
Children (ages 3–12): $20.95 USD
Children (ages 2 and under): Free

Description: The Tennessee Aquarium in Chattanooga is a top-rated destination featuring two distinct buildings dedicated to freshwater and saltwater exhibits. The aquarium is designed to provide an engaging experience, starting from the top and descending through various levels, which ensures visitors see everything without missing exhibits. The freshwater building showcases a diverse array of aquatic life from rivers and lakes, while the saltwater building features oceanic species, including large sharks and vibrant coral reefs.

The aquarium is well-equipped for accessibility and offers numerous interactive exhibits, such as touch tanks where visitors can interact with rays. Additionally, there are educational displays throughout the facility, enhancing the learning experience. The butterfly exhibit provides a unique change of pace, offering a glimpse into the lives of these delicate creatures.

Guests can enjoy well-maintained outdoor areas with beautiful landscaping, including water features and a giant staircase arch. The facility also includes an IMAX theater showing nature films, which can be a fun addition to the visit. The aquarium is conveniently located near parking areas, though a small fee applies. A free shuttle service is available for visitors who prefer not to walk back to their accommodations.

Nearby Attractions:
- Chattanooga River Market: A local market with various food and craft stalls.
- Coolidge Park: Offers scenic views and a carousel, located a short distance from the aquarium.

Important Information for Visitors:
- It is recommended to purchase tickets in advance to avoid long lines, particularly on weekends.
- Parking is available for a small fee, and the facility is accessible by free shuttle from nearby locations.
- The aquarium's layout features two separate buildings, so allocate ample time to explore both the freshwater and saltwater exhibits.
- The butterfly exhibit and touch tanks are particularly popular, so consider visiting these areas early to avoid crowds.
- The aquarium is open daily except Thursdays when it closes early at 2 pm.

Grand Ole Opry

Location: 600 Opry Mills Dr, Nashville, TN 37214, United States

Plus Code:
6845+P5 Nashville, Tennessee, USA

Website: www.opry.com

Contact: +1 615-871-6779

Opening Hours:
Monday to Friday: 10am – 5pm
Saturday to Sunday: 10am – 4pm

Description:
The Grand Ole Opry is a premier venue for country music in Nashville, renowned for its historic charm and iconic performances. As the longest-running radio show in history, it has hosted legendary artists since its opening in 1925. The venue offers a memorable experience with its well-designed acoustics and comfortable padded church pews. Visitors are advised to arrive early, as wait times for shows can be up to an hour. Parking is available for a fee of $20, or you can opt for a taxi drop-off. Food and drink, including pizza and popcorn, are available for purchase inside. It's highly recommended to make a reservation in advance and consider using a taxi or ride-sharing service to avoid potential traffic issues. The Opry provides a rich blend of nostalgia and top-tier entertainment, making it a must-visit for music lovers.

Admission (Ticket):
Prices vary; check the official website for current ticket rates and availability.

Nearby Attractions:
The Opry Mills Mall and the Opryland Hotel are located nearby, offering additional shopping and dining options.

Important Information for Visitors:
Arrive early to manage wait times and ensure a smooth entry. Be aware of potential traffic and ride-share challenges post-show.

Centennial Park

Location:
2500 West End Ave, Nashville, TN 37203, United States
Plus Code:
45XP+HW Nashville, Tennessee, USA
Website: www.nashville.gov
Contact: +1 615-862-8400
Opening Hours:
Monday to Sunday: 6am – 11pm
Description:
Centennial Park is a vast urban green space in Nashville offering a diverse range of activities and scenic spots. The park features expansive lawns perfect for picnics, leisurely strolls, and relaxation. A highlight is the full-scale replica of the Parthenon, which houses an art gallery with notable works, including pieces by Thomas Moran, and a striking statue of Athena. The park is well-maintained, safe, and includes a lake, playgrounds, and beautifully landscaped gardens that provide a serene escape from the city's hustle and bustle. Admission to the Parthenon is approximately $10. This park is highly recommended for its blend of natural beauty, historical interest, and recreational facilities.

Admission (Ticket):
Parthenon entry fee: Approximately $10 (check the official website for current rates)

Nearby Attractions:
- **The Vanderbilt University Campus:** Adjacent to the park, featuring beautiful architecture and gardens.
- **The Frist Art Museum:** Located a short drive away, offering diverse art exhibitions and educational programs.

Important Information for Visitors:
The park is open daily with no entry fee for general access. For those visiting the Parthenon, be aware of the admission fee and check for any special exhibitions or events that might be occurring.

Belle Meade Historic Site & Winery

Location:
5025 Harding Pike, Nashville, TN 37205, United States
Plus Code:
443P+X4 Nashville, Tennessee, USA
Website: www.visitbellemeade.com
Contact: +1 615-356-0501
Opening Hours:
Monday to Sunday: 9am – 5pm
Description:
Belle Meade Historic Site & Winery offers a rich blend of history and relaxation set in a beautifully maintained estate. Visitors can explore the historic mansion on a guided tour that delves into the fascinating history of the plantation. The tour includes insights into the mansion's past and concludes with a wine tasting, featuring the estate's wines. The grounds are expansive and well-kept, providing a pleasant environment to enjoy the wine purchased from the site. The property's picturesque setting offers a serene escape from the city's busyness. Reservations are recommended for the tours.

Nearby Attractions:
- **Cheekwood Estate & Gardens:** A nearby estate offering botanical gardens and art exhibitions.
- **The Parthenon:** A full-scale replica of the Parthenon located in Centennial Park.

Important Information for Visitors:
It is highly recommended to make reservations in advance for the mansion tours. Wine tastings are included with the tour, and visitors can enjoy purchased wine on the property. Check the official website for updates on ticket pricing and tour availability.

Country Music Hall of Fame and Museum

Location:
222 Rep. John Lewis Way S, Nashville, TN 37203, United States
Plus Code:
565F+8G Nashville, Tennessee, USA
Website:
www.countrymusichalloffame.org
Contact: +1 615-416-2001
Opening Hours:
Monday to Sunday: 9am – 5pm
Description:
The Country Music Hall of Fame and Museum is a must-visit destination for country music enthusiasts and those interested in American music history. The museum offers an extensive collection of memorabilia, including artifacts from both legendary and contemporary artists. Exhibits cover various eras of country music, from its origins to the present day, and include interactive displays and hands-on activities. Visitors can also enjoy live performances in the museum's auditorium. Tickets are approximately $30, with discounts available for military personnel, first responders, and AAA members. The museum's gift shop offers a selection of unique items, including reasonably priced Christmas ornaments. Guests are allowed to bring in their own water bottles, though purchasing refreshments on-site is also an option.
Admission (Ticket):
Approximately $30; discounts available for military, first responders, and AAA members.
Nearby Attractions:
- **Ryman Auditorium:** Known as the "Mother Church of Country Music," it offers historical tours and live performances.
- **Johnny Cash Museum:** Located nearby, this museum provides a comprehensive look at the life and career of Johnny Cash.

Important Information for Visitors:
Reservations are not required, but it is advisable to purchase tickets in advance, especially during peak times. The museum allows guests to bring their own water bottles, which can be helpful during extended visits.

Dolly's Tennessee Mountain Home

Location:
2700 Dollywood Parks Blvd, Pigeon Forge, TN 37863, United States

Plus Code:
QFV8+98 Pigeon Forge, Tennessee, USA

Website: www.dollywood.com

Contact: +1 800-365-5996

Opening Hours:
Monday to Sunday: 10am – 9pm (Hours may vary; check the website for current times)

Description:
Dolly's Tennessee Mountain Home is a charming attraction located within Dollywood theme park, offering a glimpse into Dolly Parton's early life through a meticulously recreated version of her childhood home. This immersive experience is part of the larger Dollywood complex, which features a variety of shows, rides, and themed attractions. Visitors can explore the replica home and gain insights into Dolly Parton's background and heritage. The park itself is known for its vibrant floral displays, thrilling roller coasters, and festive events such as the Christmas lights and drone light show. While food can be pricey, alternatives like the trolley from Patriot Park provide a cost-effective transportation option. Tickets often come with military and senior discounts, and various pass options are available for extended visits.

Admission (Ticket):
Check the official website for current pricing and discount information. Ticket options include all-day passes and special packages.

Nearby Attractions:
- **Great Smoky Mountains National Park:** Offering beautiful natural scenery and outdoor activities.
- **Gatlinburg Space Needle:** An observation tower providing panoramic views of the surrounding area.

Important Information for Visitors:
It is recommended to purchase tickets in advance and consider using the trolley service from Patriot Park to avoid higher parking fees. Be prepared for potential wait times during peak hours, and take advantage

of water and sunscreen for comfort. If visiting during peak seasons or special events, check the website for up-to-date information on hours and ticket availability.

SOAR Adventure Tower

Location:
3794 Carothers Pkwy, Franklin, TN 37067, United States
Plus Code:
W55G+8H Franklin, Tennessee, USA
Website: www.soaradventure.com
Contact:
+1 615-721-5103
Opening Hours:
Thursday: 1pm – 9pm
Friday: 1pm – 10pm
Saturday: 10am – 10pm
Sunday: 10am – 8pm
Monday: 1pm – 9pm
Tuesday: 1pm – 9pm
Wednesday: 10am – 9pm

Description:
SOAR Adventure Tower is an engaging destination offering a range of activities for all ages, including a ropes course, mini-golf, and various team-building challenges. The facility is designed to provide wholesome fun in a safe environment, with activities tailored to entertain both young children and adults. The ropes course is a highlight, offering a fun and challenging experience that can keep kids entertained for hours. While the food options are limited, the venue's amenities and activities make it a great spot for family outings, birthday parties, and corporate events. The staff is known for their friendliness and attentiveness, ensuring a pleasant visit for all guests. Reservations are recommended for large groups or special events.

Nearby Attractions:
- **CoolSprings Galleria:** A large shopping mall with a variety of retail stores and dining options.

- **Franklin Historic District:** Offering charming shops, restaurants, and historical sites.

Important Information for Visitors:
No reservations are needed for general admission, but they are recommended for large groups or special events. The facility provides a thorough safety briefing for all participants on the ropes course. Be sure to check the website for up-to-date information on hours and ticket prices before visiting.

Nashville Shores

Location:
4001 Bell Rd, Hermitage, TN 37076, United States
Plus Code:
595W+72 Hermitage, Nashville, TN, USA
Website: www.nashvilleshores.com
Contact: +1 615-889-7050
Opening Hours:
Thursday: Closed
Friday: Closed
Saturday: 10am – 6pm
Sunday: 10am – 6pm
Monday: Closed
Tuesday: Closed
Wednesday: Closed

Description:
Nashville Shores, located at the Nashville Shores Lakeside Resort, offers a variety of water-based attractions including slides, a lazy river, and a lakeside obstacle course. The park provides a family-friendly environment with clean pools and friendly staff. Guests are advised to bring their own food and use the picnic areas due to long wait times at food courts. While some amenities like bathrooms and showers may require more attention, the overall experience is enjoyable. The park's attractions are designed to cater to different age groups, ensuring fun for everyone. Visitors should note that the park has a $15 parking fee and an additional $15 locker fee. For a more budget-friendly visit, arriving after 4 pm may reduce costs. It is recommended to check for any maintenance closures or restrictions on rides before your visit.

Admission (Ticket):
Check the official website for current pricing and ticket options.
Nearby Attractions:
- **Opry Mills Mall:** A large shopping mall with diverse dining and retail options.
- **The Hermitage:** The historic home of President Andrew Jackson, offering guided tours and historical exhibits.

Important Information for Visitors:
Reservations are not required but are recommended for special events or large groups. The park's food and beverage options can be limited and expensive, so planning ahead is advisable. The park's layout may lead to longer waits at some attractions, so consider visiting during less busy hours for a more relaxed experience.

Walk of Fame Park

Location:
121 4th Ave S, Nashville, TN 37201, United States
Plus Code:
565F+M6 Nashville, Tennessee, USA
Website: www.visitmusiccity.com
Contact: +1 800-657-6910
Opening Hours:
Open 24 hours
Description:
Walk of Fame Park is a free, outdoor attraction in downtown Nashville, conveniently located near the Country Music Hall of Fame and the stadium. This park features commemorative stars embedded in the pavement, honoring influential figures in the music industry, including legends like Elvis Presley, Dolly Parton, and Johnny Cash. It offers a casual and quick stop for those exploring the downtown area. While the park itself may not be elaborate, it provides a meaningful and enjoyable way to connect with the musical heritage of Nashville. It's a great spot for photos and a brief respite while exploring the city's vibrant music scene.
Nearby Attractions:

- **Country Music Hall of Fame and Museum:** A comprehensive museum dedicated to the history of country music.
- **Ryman Auditorium:** A historic venue known for its role in country music and live performances.

Important Information for Visitors:
The park is open 24 hours and is a convenient, free attraction for visitors. It's best enjoyed as part of a broader exploration of downtown Nashville, particularly if you're visiting nearby music landmarks.

Nashville Public Square Park

Location:
Union St & 3rd Ave N, Nashville, TN 37201, United States
Plus Code:
568C+JP Nashville, Tennessee, USA
Website:
www.nashvilledowntown.com
Contact: +1 615-743-3090
Opening Hours:
- **Thursday to Sunday:** 5:05 am – 11:00 pm
- **Monday to Wednesday:** 5:05 am – 11:00 pm

Description:
Nashville Public Square Park is a lively and scenic riverfront park located near Broadway and the pedestrian bridge to Nissan Stadium. It's an excellent spot for enjoying the city's vibrant atmosphere, particularly during events like fireworks displays. The park features a grassy area ideal for relaxing, though it lacks dedicated picnic areas and playgrounds. While restrooms are not directly within the park, they are available in nearby local businesses. The park is generally dog-friendly outside of major events and is situated in a well-monitored area, enhancing its safety. It's also conveniently located near paid parking garages, with free parking options available on weekends at government-owned facilities.

Nearby Attractions:

- **Broadway:** A bustling street known for its live music venues and entertainment.
- **Nissan Stadium:** Home to the Tennessee Titans and a venue for major events.

Important Information for Visitors:
The park is open daily from early morning to late evening, providing a great spot for a break while exploring downtown Nashville. It is a good place to enjoy some quiet time or catch local events. Keep an eye out for dog waste, as not all dog owners may pick up after their pets.

Radnor Lake State Park

Location:
1160 Otter Creek Rd, Nashville, TN 37220, United States
Plus Code:
357R+64 Nashville, Tennessee, USA
Website:
www.tnstateparks.com
Contact:
+1 888-867-2757
Opening Hours:
- **Thursday to Wednesday:** 6:00 am – 6:00 pm

Description:
Radnor Lake State Park offers a serene escape from the hustle of Nashville with its well-maintained trails and peaceful natural surroundings. It is an excellent destination for nature enthusiasts and hikers, featuring a beautiful 3-mile loop around the lake, where you might spot wildlife such as deer, turtles, and various bird species. The park is ideal for a quiet day hike or a relaxing walk amidst nature. However, it's important to note that the park is not dog-friendly, with restrictions limiting pets to paved areas only. Parking can be limited, so it's advisable to arrive early. Restrooms are available at the park, enhancing visitor convenience. The park provides a wonderful contrast to the nearby city life, offering a tranquil environment perfect for disconnecting and enjoying the beauty of the natural world.

Nearby Attractions:
- **Vanderbilt University:** Nearby educational institution with a beautiful campus.

- **Nashville Metro Parks:** Additional parks and recreational areas in the vicinity.

Important Information for Visitors:
- Parking is restricted to designated areas; avoid driving up the hill as it leads to a dead end.
- Limited parking availability, so early arrival is recommended.
- Dogs are not allowed on trails; only paved roads are accessible for pets.

Madame Tussauds Nashville

Location:
Opry Mills, 515 Opry Mills Dr, Nashville, TN 37214, United States

Plus Code:
6834+W9 Nashville, Tennessee, USA

Website: www.madametussauds.com

Contact: +1 615-485-4867

Opening Hours:
- **Thursday to Saturday:** 10:00 am – 8:00 pm
- **Sunday:** 11:00 am – 6:00 pm
- **Monday to Wednesday:** 10:00 am – 8:00 pm

Description:
Madame Tussauds Nashville offers an engaging experience with lifelike wax figures of music stars and celebrities. Located in Opry Mills, this attraction provides a fun, interactive visit perfect for all ages. The museum is well-maintained, with figures and exhibits that showcase a variety of genres, from country to pop. The space is designed for easy navigation, allowing visitors to explore at their own pace. Tickets are valid all day, and the attraction is card-only for payments. The venue is LGBTQ+ friendly and features friendly staff, including artists who may be present to share insights. The location within Opry Mills provides convenient dining options and additional activities, making it a great indoor option, especially on rainy days.

Nearby Attractions:
- **Opry Mills Mall:** A large shopping and entertainment complex with numerous dining and retail options.

- **Grand Ole Opry:** Famous for its live country music performances, located nearby.

Important Information for Visitors:
- No reservations required, but it is recommended to check availability, especially on weekends.
- The attraction can get crowded, so visiting during off-peak hours may enhance the experience.
- The museum accepts card payments only.

Nashville WhatLiftsYou Wings Mural

Location: 302 11th Ave S, Nashville, TN 37203, United States
Plus Code: 5638+H9 Nashville, Tennessee, USA
Website:
www.kelseymontagueart.com

Opening Hours: Open 24 hours

Description: The Nashville WhatLiftsYou Wings Mural, created by artist Kelsey Montague, is a popular photo spot located in the trendy Gulch area. This vibrant and iconic mural features large, colorful wings that invite visitors to strike a pose and create memorable photographs. Situated near various upscale shops and dining options, it offers a perfect backdrop for social media photos. While it's a great spot for spontaneous photo sessions, be aware that it can get busy, especially during peak seasons. Lines for photos may range from a few minutes to half an hour, so visiting earlier in the day is advisable to avoid long waits. The mural is easily accessible and offers a unique experience in Nashville's artsy district.

Admission (Ticket): Free
Nearby Attractions: The mural is located in The Gulch, a vibrant neighborhood known for its trendy shops, upscale dining, and other artistic murals. The area also offers a range of cafes and restaurants for a complete outing experience.

Important Information for Visitors: The mural is open 24 hours, making it convenient for early morning or late night photo sessions. It is recommended to visit earlier in the day to avoid long lines, especially on weekends. Parking is available in nearby garages, and the area is walkable with various amenities within reach.

Old Stone Fort State Archaeological Park

Location: 732 Stone Fort Dr, Manchester, TN 37355, United States
Plus Code: FVPW+GW Manchester, Tennessee, USA
Website: www.tnstateparks.com
Contact: +1 888-867-2757
Opening Hours: Monday to Sunday: 8am – 4:30pm
Description: Old Stone Fort State Archaeological Park offers visitors a rich blend of natural beauty and historical significance. The park is renowned for its Native American ceremonial mounds and scenic hiking trails that lead to picturesque waterfalls. The trails, though occasionally needing maintenance, offer a peaceful escape into nature with opportunities to experience the calming sound of flowing water. The park includes a museum where visitors can learn about the area's history, and well-maintained restrooms are available. The park is dog-friendly, although there is no designated dog park. It provides ample picnic spaces and clean facilities. For those planning to hike, it is advisable to bring appropriate footwear and be prepared for natural elements, such as potential wildlife. The park is ideal for history enthusiasts, nature lovers, and those seeking a tranquil environment.
Admission (Ticket): Free
Nearby Attractions: The park is situated near Manchester, Tennessee, where additional recreational and historical sites can be explored.
Important Information for Visitors: The park is open daily with consistent hours throughout the week. Be prepared for natural conditions by bringing suitable gear for hiking and water activities. The

park offers shaded picnic areas and clean facilities, making it a comfortable destination for families and individuals.

Cannonsburgh Village

Location: 312 S Front St, Murfreesboro, TN 37129, United States
Plus Code: RJV3+GG Murfreesboro, Tennessee, USA

Website: www.murfreesborotn.gov
Contact: +1 615-890-0355
Opening Hours:
- Thursday: 9am – 6pm
- Friday: 9am – 6pm
- Saturday: 9am – 4pm
- Sunday: 1pm – 4pm
- Monday: Closed
- Tuesday: 9am – 6pm
- Wednesday: 9am – 6pm

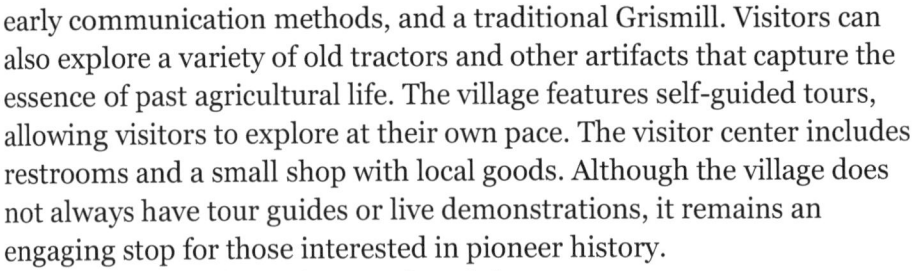

Description: Cannonsburgh Village offers a charming glimpse into historical rural life with its collection of restored buildings and exhibits. Highlights include a historic telephone switchboard with a bed for the operator, providing insight into early communication methods, and a traditional Grismill. Visitors can also explore a variety of old tractors and other artifacts that capture the essence of past agricultural life. The village features self-guided tours, allowing visitors to explore at their own pace. The visitor center includes restrooms and a small shop with local goods. Although the village does not always have tour guides or live demonstrations, it remains an engaging stop for those interested in pioneer history.
Admission (Ticket): $5 USD for adults
Nearby Attractions: Cannonsburgh Village is located in Murfreesboro, where additional historical and cultural sites can be explored.
Important Information for Visitors: The village is closed on Mondays. For the best experience, consider visiting on days when the

village is fully staffed and check for any special events or activities. Restrooms are available across the grounds and in the visitor center.

Great Smoky Mountains National Park

Plus Code: JC7W+6P Gatlinburg, Tennessee, USA
Website: www.nps.gov
Contact: +1 865-436-1200
Opening Hours: Open 24 hours
Description: Great Smoky Mountains National Park is renowned for its breathtaking natural beauty and diverse wildlife. Visitors can enjoy stunning panoramic views from numerous scenic overlooks, lush forests, vibrant wildflowers, and pristine streams. The park features an extensive network of trails suitable for various levels of hiking experience. Wildlife enthusiasts may encounter turkeys, deer, and occasionally bears. The park's visitor centers provide helpful information, restrooms, and a range of souvenirs and merchandise. Given its popularity, especially on weekends, it is advisable to visit during weekdays to avoid heavy crowds and traffic. The park offers restrooms at midpoint locations along the loop and near the visitor centers.
Admission (Ticket): Free entry
Nearby Attractions: The park's proximity to Gatlinburg offers additional activities and attractions, including scenic drives, cultural sites, and local dining options.
Important Information for Visitors: The park is open 24 hours, but certain facilities may have limited hours. Be prepared for heavy traffic and crowds on weekends. It is highly recommended to plan visits during weekdays and to check for any alerts or park updates before arrival.

2nd Avenue Historic District

Location: 2nd Ave N, Nashville, TN 37201, United States

Plus Code: 566F+CW Nashville, Tennessee, USA

Website: www.nashvilledowntown.com

Opening Hours: Monday to Sunday: 10am – 3am

Description: The 2nd Avenue Historic District is a vibrant area in Nashville known for its lively atmosphere and local charm. This district is a hotspot for live music, eclectic dining, and a dynamic nightlife experience. Visitors can enjoy a variety of musical performances, from house bands to solo acts, in numerous venues. The district is particularly popular among younger crowds but offers something for all ages. It is recommended to visit during the evening for a lively experience, though daytime visits can also be enjoyable. The area can become crowded, and prices may be higher, especially in peak hours. Safety measures are in place with police monitoring the area during late hours.

Admission (Ticket): Free

Nearby Attractions: The district's central location offers easy access to other Nashville landmarks and attractions, including Broadway's music venues and nearby restaurants.

Important Information for Visitors: The district is open late into the night, making it ideal for evening entertainment. Be mindful of increased prices and potential crowds. Safety can be a concern in the area after dark, so it's advisable to remain vigilant and stay within well-lit and populated areas.

Stones River National Battlefield

Location: 3501 Old Nashville Hwy, Murfreesboro, TN 37129, United States
Plus Code: VHG9+CM Murfreesboro, Tennessee, USA
Website: www.nps.gov/stri
Contact: +1 615-893-9501
Opening Hours: Monday to Sunday: 9am – 5pm
Description: Stones River National Battlefield offers a profound historical experience centered around the American Civil War battle fought on this site. Visitors can explore the battlefield through self-guided or mobile app tours, which provide detailed information about key areas such as the Slaughter Pen. The battlefield is known for its well-maintained grounds, informative exhibits at the Visitors Center, and the somber yet educational atmosphere. The park features a driving tour with several stops that offer insights into the historical significance of each location. The site includes a separate picnic area, adequate restrooms, and dog-friendly paths, though pets should be kept away during live musket demonstrations. Entry to the battlefield is free, making it an accessible and valuable destination for history enthusiasts.
Admission (Ticket): Free
Nearby Attractions: The nearby cemetery across from the Visitors Center adds a somber reflection on the battlefield's history.
Important Information for Visitors: The park can be busy on weekends, so visiting on a weekday might provide a more serene experience. The area is equipped with sufficient parking and facilities. Ensure to check for any live demonstrations or events that may affect accessibility. The interpretive center is highly recommended for a comprehensive understanding of the battlefield's history.

Carter House

Location: 1140 Columbia Ave, Franklin, TN 37064, United States
Plus Code: W48G+RJ Franklin, Tennessee, USA
Website: www.boft.org
Contact: +1 615-791-1861
Opening Hours:
- **Thursday**: 9am – 5pm
- **Friday**: 9am – 5pm
- **Saturday**: 9am – 5pm
- **Sunday**: 10am – 5pm
- **Monday**: 9am – 5pm
- **Tuesday**: 9am – 5pm
- **Wednesday**: 9am – 5pm

Description: Carter House is a significant historical site known for its role in the Battle of Franklin during the American Civil War. Visitors can explore the house and its basement, which served as a shelter during the battle. The property showcases visible damage from the gunfire and contains artifacts like General Cox's field desk. Tours provide in-depth historical context and personal stories related to the battle. The house is an important stop for those interested in Civil War history and is recommended to be visited before the nearby Carnton House for a more comprehensive experience. Note that photography is not allowed inside the house, but the exterior and grounds are photographable.

Admission (Ticket): $16–20

Nearby Attractions: Carnton House, another key historical site in Franklin, is located nearby.

Important Information for Visitors: Reservations are recommended, especially during peak times. The tour is highly informative and typically lasts around an hour. The house will undergo some restoration work to better reflect the historical colors of the period.

Treetop Adventure Park at Nashville Shores

Location: Nashville Shores, Hermitage, TN 37076, United States
Plus Code: 595W+8J Hermitage, Nashville, TN, USA
Website: www.nashvilleshores.com
Contact: +1 615-889-7806
Opening Hours:
- **Thursday**: Closed
- **Friday**: Closed
- **Saturday**: 10am – 2pm
- **Sunday**: 10am – 2pm
- **Monday**: Closed
- **Tuesday**: Closed
- **Wednesday**: Closed

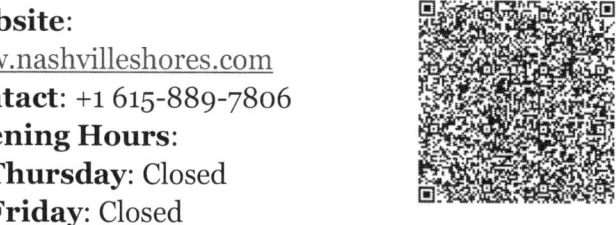

Description: Treetop Adventure Park, located at Nashville Shores Lakeside Resort, offers an exhilarating experience with its challenging obstacle courses and zip lines. The park is praised for its friendly and supportive staff, including notable instructors like Jay, who provide guidance and encouragement throughout the adventure. The courses are designed for those with some upper body strength and balance, featuring a mix of ropes and zip lines. Younger children can enjoy a large playground below the kids' course. Note that the experience is physically demanding and might not suit beginners or those looking for a more relaxed activity. It's recommended to buy tickets in advance to avoid higher on-site prices, and reservations are advised due to potential wait times.

Admission (Ticket): $31+

Nearby Attractions: Nashville Shores Lakeside Resort, which includes additional recreational activities and amenities.

Important Information for Visitors: The park is closed on weekdays and operates only on weekends, with limited hours. Reservations are recommended, and it's advised to check for a demonstration of the course before starting. The park is more suited for athletic individuals due to the physical demands of the obstacle courses.

Cumberland Caverns

Location: 1437 Cumberland Caverns Rd, McMinnville, TN 37110, United States
Plus Code: M888+FR McMinnville, Tennessee, USA
Website: www.cumberlandcaverns.com
Contact: +1 931-668-4396
Opening Hours:
- **Thursday**: 9am – 4pm
- **Friday**: 9am – 5pm
- **Saturday**: 9am – 5pm
- **Sunday**: 9am – 5:30pm
- **Monday**: 9am – 5:30pm
- **Tuesday**: 9am – 4pm
- **Wednesday**: 9am – 4pm

Description: Cumberland Caverns offers a captivating underground experience with various tours showcasing its stunning natural formations. The Discovery Walking Tour, which lasts about 90 minutes, is highly recommended for its value and comprehensive exploration of the cave. Visitors are guided through beautiful rooms such as the Volcano Room and are introduced to fascinating stories about the cave's history. The caverns maintain a steady 58°F year-round, so visitors should dress comfortably but not overly warm. For a more adventurous experience, the Higgenbotham Hollow tour provides an introduction to spelunking, led by knowledgeable and personable guides. The staff, including guides like Tom, Vera, Grant, and Derek, are praised for their informative and friendly approach. Reservations are recommended for all tours, and it's noted that the facility is LGBTQ+ friendly.

Admission (Ticket): $100 for a 90-minute Discovery Walking Tour (prices vary by tour)

Nearby Attractions: The scenic drive to the caverns from Nashville is noted for its ease and beauty.

Important Information for Visitors: The caves are a steady 58°F year-round, so comfortable clothing is advised. Reservations are recommended, and there are various tours to choose from depending on your interest and fitness level. The facility is accommodating for a range of physical abilities.

Rock Island State Park

Location: 82 Beach Rd, Rock Island, TN 38581, United States
Plus Code: R965+57 Rock Island, Tennessee, USA
Website: www.tnstateparks.com
Contact: +1 888-867-2757
Opening Hours: The park is open daily, but specific hours for certain activities or facilities may vary.
Description: Rock Island State Park is renowned for its stunning natural beauty and outdoor recreational opportunities. Visitors can explore scenic trails, enjoy climbing and swimming in natural rock pools, and witness breathtaking waterfalls. The park features a blend of natural and man-made elements, such as the Twin Falls, which are influenced by a dam. The park offers various activities including hiking, kayaking, and beach swimming. For an immersive experience, visitors can rent cabins, which are noted for their spaciousness and comfort. The park also provides picnic areas and a serene environment for relaxation and exploration. The main entrance is recommended for easy access to the park's central attractions. Be prepared with hiking and water shoes, and bring sufficient snacks and drinks.
Admission: The park is generally free to enter, but certain activities or rentals may incur additional fees.
Nearby Attractions: The park's diverse landscapes and water features offer plenty of exploration opportunities, including scenic drives and additional hiking trails.
Important Information for Visitors:
- **Safety Note**: Be aware of dam-related alarms, especially near the Twin Falls, which indicate water flow changes.

- **Facilities**: The park has cabins and picnic areas, but bring your own food and water. The park is well-suited for visitors of all ages and physical abilities.
- **What to Bring**: Comfortable hiking shoes, water shoes, snacks, and plenty of drinks.

The Chattanooga Zoo at Warner Park

Location: 301 N Holtzclaw Ave, Chattanooga, TN 37404, United States
Plus Code: 2PV9+35 Chattanooga, Tennessee, USA
Website: www.chattzoo.org
Contact: +1 423-697-1322
Opening Hours:
- **Thursday to Sunday**: 9 am – 5 pm
- **Monday to Wednesday**: Closed

Description: The Chattanooga Zoo at Warner Park is a well-maintained, smaller zoo offering a variety of animal exhibits and interactive experiences. Visitors can enjoy viewing animals in clean and well-kept environments, with some unique species not commonly found in other zoos. The zoo provides ample indoor facilities to escape the heat and is equipped with fans for added comfort. The zoo features a popular Red Panda experience, where guests can interact with these charming animals. Other highlights include a recent Africa exhibit and educational encounters such as the chimp caretaker experience. The zoo's layout is easy to navigate, and parking is convenient. Although small, it offers a fulfilling visit with plenty of photo opportunities and a well-stocked gift shop.

Admission: Generally affordable, with special experiences like the Red Panda encounter available for an additional fee.

Nearby Attractions: The zoo is part of a larger park area, and Chattanooga offers additional attractions such as the Tennessee Aquarium and Lookout Mountain.

Important Information for Visitors:
- **Reservation**: It is recommended to book tickets in advance, especially for special experiences.

- **Facilities**: There are indoor cooling areas and fan stations. The zoo is family-friendly with amenities for children.
- **What to Bring**: Comfortable clothing, sunscreen, and a camera for the many photo opportunities.

Tennessee State Museum

Location: 1000 Rosa L Parks Blvd, Nashville, TN 37208, United States
Plus Code: 56C5+XX Nashville, Tennessee, USA
Website: tnmuseum.org
Contact: +1 615-741-2692
Opening Hours:
- **Thursday to Saturday**: 10 am – 5 pm
- **Sunday**: 1 pm – 5 pm
- **Monday**: Closed
- **Tuesday to Wednesday**: 10 am – 5 pm

Description: The Tennessee State Museum offers a comprehensive and immersive exploration of the state's history from prehistoric times to the present day. The museum is spacious and features a range of exhibits that are both educational and visually engaging. Highlights include detailed galleries, interactive touch-screen tables, and informative films that provide context for the exhibits. The museum's collection covers various aspects of Tennessee's history, including its cultural and musical heritage. It also has a well-regarded gallery dedicated to Tennessee music. The museum is free of charge and includes amenities such as a store, and it's conveniently located near Bicentennial Mall State Park, the Nashville Farmers Market, and the Nashville Sound Baseball Stadium.
Admission: Free
Nearby Attractions: Bicentennial Mall State Park, Nashville Farmers Market, Nashville Sound Baseball Stadium
Important Information for Visitors:
- **Reservation**: No reservation is required.
- **Facilities**: The museum is wheelchair and stroller accessible, with wide open spaces and large elevators.

- **What to Bring**: Comfortable clothing and a camera for capturing exhibits and views from the balcony.

Adventure Science Center

Location: 800 Fort Negley Blvd, Nashville, TN 37203, United States
Plus Code: 46WF+JR Nashville, Tennessee, USA
Website: adventuresci.org
Contact: +1 615-862-5160
Opening Hours:
- **Monday to Thursday**: Closed
- **Friday**: 9 am – 5 pm
- **Saturday**: 10 am – 5 pm
- **Sunday**: 12 pm – 5 pm

Description: The Adventure Science Center is a dynamic and interactive destination perfect for families and visitors of all ages. The center features a variety of hands-on exhibits and activities that engage visitors in the exploration of science and technology. Highlights include the Body Works area with its laser game, where visitors can experience the thrill of working as good or bad bacteria. The solar system display and the planetarium offer awe-inspiring educational experiences, although the planetarium may be closed for renovations at times. There are also craft stations where children can create items like bouncy balls. Despite occasional closures or operational limitations, the center provides a fun and educational experience that can be enjoyed by repeat visits.

Admission: Prices vary; check the website for current rates and discounts.

Nearby Attractions: Consider exploring nearby parks and museums to make a day of it.

Important Information for Visitors:
- **Reservation**: Recommended, especially during peak times or for specific exhibits.
- **Facilities**: The center is well-equipped for families, including interactive exhibits and craft stations. A map may be helpful to

navigate the exhibits, and checking the website for current operations is advised.
- **What to Bring**: Comfortable clothing and a willingness to engage with interactive exhibits.

Cheekwood Estate & Gardens

Location: 1200 Forrest Park Dr, Nashville, TN 37205, United States
Plus Code: 34QF+9J Nashville, Tennessee, USA
Website: www.cheekwood.org
Contact: +1 615-356-8000
Opening Hours:
- Thursday to Friday: 9am – 5pm
- Saturday to Sunday: 9am – 5pm
- Monday: Closed
- Tuesday to Wednesday: 9am – 5pm

Description: Cheekwood Estate & Gardens offers a stunning experience with its expansive grounds and well-maintained gardens. Visitors can enjoy a leisurely stroll through various themed gardens, explore art installations, and take in the picturesque natural scenery. The estate includes a historic mansion with a range of exhibits and is perfect for picnics, relaxation, or family outings. Notable features include seasonal art installations and a variety of outdoor spaces ideal for nature enthusiasts. Visitors are encouraged to bring their own refreshments for picnicking. Onsite amenities include a café, though some prefer bringing their own lunch. A hat, sunscreen, and water are recommended for a comfortable visit. Blue Star Museum Program offers free admission for active military members. The park is easily accessible from downtown Nashville, approximately a 20-minute drive.

Nearby Attractions:
- Downtown Nashville
- Nashville Farmers Market
- Bicentennial Mall State Park

Important Information for Visitors:
- Blue Star Museum Program available for free admission to active military personnel.
- The park is open year-round, but the café is only operational during certain hours; consider bringing your own food and drinks.

The Escape Game Nashville (Downtown)

Location: 162 3rd Ave N, Nashville, TN 37201, United States
Plus Code: 567F+C5 Nashville, Tennessee, USA
Website: www.theescapegame.com
Contact: +1 615-241-5609
Opening Hours:

- Monday to Sunday: 8am – 12am

Description: The Escape Game Nashville (Downtown) offers a thrilling and interactive escape room experience perfect for groups of friends, families, or couples. Located in the heart of Nashville, the facility features a range of meticulously designed escape rooms with unique themes and challenging puzzles. Each game immerses participants in a story-driven adventure, where teams must solve clues and complete tasks within a set time to "escape" the room. The venue is open daily from 8am to midnight, allowing for flexible booking times. Guests are advised to make reservations in advance, especially during peak hours. The Escape Game Nashville provides a memorable experience with friendly and attentive staff, ensuring a fun and engaging activity for visitors of all ages.
Admission (Ticket) ($): Please check the official website for current ticket prices.
Nearby Attractions:
- Broadway Street
- Country Music Hall of Fame and Museum
- Ryman Auditorium

Important Information for Visitors:
- Reservations are recommended to secure your preferred time slot.
- Participants can purchase themed merchandise and enjoy "I Escaped" stickers as a keepsake after completing the game.

Escape Experience - Nashville Escape Games (Downtown)

Location: 501 Union St, Nashville, TN 37219, United States
Plus Code: 5679+PF Nashville, Tennessee, USA
Website: www.escapeexperience.com
Contact: +1 615-891-7929
Opening Hours:
- Monday to Wednesday: 11am – 10pm
- Thursday: 11am – 10pm
- Friday: 9am – 11:45pm
- Saturday: 9am – 11:45pm
- Sunday: 12pm – 10pm

Description: Escape Experience - Nashville Escape Games offers an engaging and immersive escape room adventure in downtown Nashville. Located on the first floor of the 501 Union Building, this venue features a variety of escape rooms with intricate themes and challenging puzzles designed to test your problem-solving skills. The facility is open seven days a week, with extended hours on weekends. Guests can choose from different escape experiences, each with its own storyline and set of challenges. The venue is praised for its well-designed rooms and enthusiastic staff, providing a memorable and enjoyable experience for both newcomers and escape room enthusiasts. Reservations are highly recommended to ensure availability.

Nearby Attractions:
- Ryman Auditorium
- Broadway Street
- Country Music Hall of Fame and Museum

Important Information for Visitors:
- Advanced reservations are recommended, especially during peak times.
- The venue offers various themed escape rooms with different levels of difficulty.
- For the best experience, review the escape room themes and select one that matches your interest and skill level.

Memory updated

Lane Motor Museum
Location:
702 Murfreesboro Pike, Nashville, TN 37210, United States
Plus Code:
47R8+35 Nashville, Tennessee, USA
Website:
www.lanemotormuseum.org
Contact:
+1 615-742-7445
Opening Hours:
Thursday to Friday: 10am – 5pm
Saturday to Sunday: 10am – 5pm
Monday: 10am – 5pm
Closed on Tuesday and Wednesday
Description:
Lane Motor Museum is a family-owned attraction featuring an extensive collection of cars from various countries, all maintained in excellent working condition. Visitors can explore a diverse range of vehicles, from vintage classics to unique models, providing a comprehensive view of automotive history. The museum's layout includes sections that categorize cars by their origins and eras, enhancing the visitor experience. Special events such as free antique car rides and exclusive access to the museum's vault, which houses additional vehicles not on display, are periodically offered. The museum's parking garage doubles as an exhibit space, showcasing some vehicles in a creative setting. It is highly recommended to check the museum's website for updated event

schedules and any special tours. The museum is a fantastic family destination, offering an engaging experience for car enthusiasts and casual visitors alike.

Nearby Attractions:
- **The Escape Game Nashville (Downtown):** An interactive escape room experience located at 162 3rd Ave N, Nashville, TN 37201.
- **Cheekwood:** A historic estate and botanical garden located at 1200 Forrest Park Dr, Nashville, TN 37205.

Important Information for Visitors:
It is advisable to visit the museum's website for information on special events and possible changes in opening hours. Parking is available on-site, and the museum provides a unique experience with its diverse car collection and creative display setups.

Ryman Auditorium

Location:
116 5th Ave N, Nashville, TN 37219, United States
Plus Code:
566C+FJ Nashville, Tennessee, USA
Website: www.ryman.com
Contact: +1 800-733-6779
Opening Hours:
Thursday to Saturday: 9am – 4pm
Sunday to Monday: 9am – 4pm
Wednesday: 9am – 2:15pm
Closed on Tuesday
Description:
Ryman Auditorium, renowned for its historic charm and exceptional acoustics, is one of Nashville's most iconic music venues. Originally built as a church, the auditorium is celebrated for its stunning stained glass windows and beautifully preserved wooden pews. It offers an immersive experience where the sound quality enhances every performance, making every seat feel special. Visitors can enjoy a self-guided tour that provides insight into the venue's rich history and its role in shaping Nashville's musical legacy.

Special events and concerts regularly take place, with performances ranging from contemporary shows to classic country music. It is highly recommended to book tickets in advance, as shows and tours can be in high demand.

Nearby Attractions:
- **The Escape Game Nashville (Downtown):** An interactive escape room experience located at 162 3rd Ave N, Nashville, TN 37201.
- **Cheekwood:** A historic estate and botanical garden located at 1200 Forrest Park Dr, Nashville, TN 37205.
- **Lane Motor Museum:** A unique car museum located at 702 Murfreesboro Pike, Nashville, TN 37210.

Important Information for Visitors:
Reservations are recommended for both tours and performances due to high demand. Visitors should check the Ryman Auditorium's website for the latest information on tour schedules and event timings. The auditorium's seating, though historic, may be less padded than modern venues, so bringing a cushion might enhance comfort during longer performances.

Musicians Hall of Fame and Museum

Location:
401 Gay St, Nashville, TN 37219, United States

Plus Code:
5699+42 Nashville, Tennessee, USA

Website:
www.musicianshalloffame.com

Contact: +1 615-244-3263

Opening Hours:
Thursday to Saturday: 10am – 5pm
Monday to Tuesday: 10am – 5pm
Wednesday: 10am – 5pm
Closed on Sunday

Description:
The Musicians Hall of Fame and Museum, located within the Nashville Municipal Auditorium, offers an

extensive collection celebrating the artistry and contributions of musicians across various genres. The museum features interactive exhibits where visitors can explore and engage with different musical instruments, making it a hands-on experience for music enthusiasts. Highlights include detailed displays of instruments and memorabilia, as well as an introductory video that provides context about the exhibits. An audio tour is available for those interested in a more in-depth exploration of the museum's artifacts. Visitors should note that while the museum offers a rich experience, some may find the audio tour information excessive if on a tight schedule. Souvenir prices may be on the higher side, so budget accordingly. The museum is highly recommended for anyone with a passion for music history or a career in music.

Admission (Ticket) ($):
Ticket prices vary; check the official website for current pricing.

Nearby Attractions:
- **Ryman Auditorium:** A historic music venue located at 116 5th Ave N, Nashville, TN 37219.
- **The Escape Game Nashville (Downtown):** Located at 162 3rd Ave N, Nashville, TN 37201, offering interactive escape room experiences.
- **Cheekwood:** A historic estate and botanical garden at 1200 Forrest Park Dr, Nashville, TN 37205.

Important Information for Visitors:
Reservations are recommended for peak times, especially on weekends. Parking can be challenging; visitors are advised to arrive early to secure a spot. The museum offers a variety of interactive elements that may appeal to both music aficionados and casual visitors.

Boro Beach

Location:
2310 Memorial Blvd, Murfreesboro, TN 37129, United States
Plus Code:
VJP9+CC Murfreesboro, Tennessee, USA
Website: www.murfreesborotn.gov
Contact: +1 615-895-5040
Opening Hours:
Thursday to Monday: 10am – 6:30pm
Saturday: 10am – 4:30pm
Sunday: 1pm – 6pm
Closed on Tuesday and Wednesday

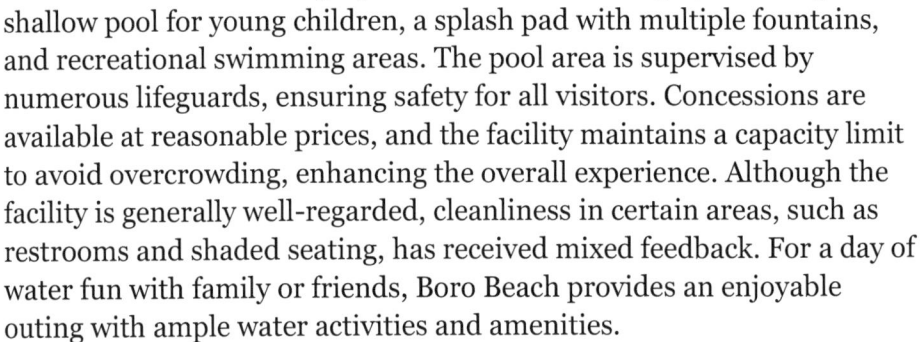

Description: Boro Beach offers a fun and family-friendly aquatic experience in Murfreesboro. The facility features various water play areas suitable for all ages, including a shallow pool for young children, a splash pad with multiple fountains, and recreational swimming areas. The pool area is supervised by numerous lifeguards, ensuring safety for all visitors. Concessions are available at reasonable prices, and the facility maintains a capacity limit to avoid overcrowding, enhancing the overall experience. Although the facility is generally well-regarded, cleanliness in certain areas, such as restrooms and shaded seating, has received mixed feedback. For a day of water fun with family or friends, Boro Beach provides an enjoyable outing with ample water activities and amenities.

Admission (Ticket) ($):
Ticket prices are available on the official website.

Nearby Attractions:
- **Lane Motor Museum:** Located at 702 Murfreesboro Pike, Nashville, TN 37210, featuring a unique collection of cars from different countries.
- **Ryman Auditorium:** Located at 116 5th Ave N, Nashville, TN 37219, a historic venue known for its impressive acoustics and performances.
- **Musicians Hall of Fame and Museum:** Situated at 401 Gay St, Nashville, TN 37219, within the Nashville Municipal Auditorium, celebrating musical history with interactive exhibits.

Important Information for Visitors:
Reservations are recommended on weekends due to the potential for capacity limits. The facility is well-suited for a range of ages, with specific areas designed for younger children. For a more enjoyable visit, consider visiting during weekdays when it is less crowded.

Charlie Daniels Park

Location: 1075 Charlie Daniels Pkwy, Mt. Juliet, TN 37122, United States
Plus Code: 6FFQ+2R Mt. Juliet, Tennessee, USA
Website: www.mjparksandrec.org
Contact: +1 615-758-6522
Opening Hours:
Monday to Sunday: 5am – 10pm
Description:

Charlie Daniels Park in Mt. Juliet is a well-maintained family-friendly park that offers a wide variety of amenities for all ages. The park features a large playground with separate areas for toddlers and older children, ensuring a safe and enjoyable experience for families. It also includes a popular free splash pad, skatepark, basketball courts, tennis courts, and picnic pavilions. The walking paths provide an excellent space for exercise, with a complete loop around the park covering about 2,000 steps. Shaded areas are available for adults to relax, and restrooms are conveniently located at both ends of the park. The park is dog-friendly, with plenty of open space for pets to enjoy.

A large parking lot is available, and the grounds are known for being clean, with staff regularly maintaining the facilities. Be aware that pavilions and certain areas may be reserved in advance, which can affect availability for spontaneous gatherings. This park is an excellent spot for outdoor recreation, family outings, and casual picnics.

Nearby Attractions:
- **Boro Beach:** Located at 2310 Memorial Blvd, Murfreesboro, TN 37129, offering water fun for the whole family with pools and a splash pad.
- **Long Hunter State Park:** A scenic park offering hiking trails, fishing, and nature walks, located a short drive away from Mt. Juliet.

Important Information for Visitors:
It's recommended to check pavilion reservations in advance if you plan on hosting an event, as some areas may be booked during peak hours. The splash pad operates seasonally, so ensure it is open during your visit.

Oaklands Mansion

Location:
900 N Maney Ave, Murfreesboro, TN 37130, United States

Plus Code:
VJ47+8X Murfreesboro, Tennessee, USA

Website:
www.oaklandsmansion.org

Contact: +1 615-893-0022

Opening Hours:
- Tuesday to Friday: 10am – 4pm
- Saturday: 10am – 5pm
- Closed on Sunday and Monday

Description: Oaklands Mansion is a historic house museum set in the heart of Murfreesboro, offering visitors a glimpse into Tennessee's rich Civil War-era history. The mansion, beautifully restored and maintained, showcases the lifestyle of its former inhabitants with period furnishings and informative exhibits in each room. Guided tours are available, providing fascinating insights into both the mansion and the lives of the enslaved people who worked there. The grounds, featuring gardens and walking paths, are perfect for a leisurely stroll, and the visitor center offers amenities such as clean restrooms and a charming gift shop.

Oaklands Mansion also serves as a popular venue for events, including community gatherings, weddings, and educational programs. The venue's professional staff ensures seamless event planning, and its scenic setting provides an elegant backdrop for special occasions. Photography is allowed inside the mansion, and the spacious parking area can accommodate large groups.

Admission (Ticket) ($):
- Adult: $15
- Seniors (65+): $12
- Students: $10
- Children under 6: Free

Nearby Attractions:
- **Cannonsburgh Village**: A recreated Southern village showcasing life from the 1800s, located just a short drive away.
- **Stones River National Battlefield**: A Civil War battlefield offering tours and historical insights, situated nearby.

Important Information for Visitors:
Advance reservations are recommended, especially during peak times or when special events are being held. Oaklands Mansion frequently hosts local events, so it's advisable to check the website or call ahead to confirm availability.

Tennessee Tornado

Location:
2700 Dollywood Parks Blvd, Pigeon Forge, TN 37863, United States (Located in Dollywood)
Plus Code: QFVC+8F Pigeon Forge, Tennessee, USA

Website: www.dollywood.com
Contact: +1 800-365-5996
Opening Hours:
- Friday: 10am – 7pm
- Saturday: 10am – 7pm
- Sunday: 10am – 8pm
- Monday: 10am – 7pm
- Wednesday: 10am – 7pm
- Closed on Tuesday and Thursday

Description: The Tennessee Tornado is a thrilling steel roller coaster located in Dollywood, offering an unforgettable experience for adrenaline seekers. Opened in 1999 and designed by Arrow Dynamics, this coaster takes riders on an intense journey through mountainous terrain. With a maximum speed of 63 mph and a height of 163 feet, the ride starts with an epic first drop that delivers exhilarating airtime as you plummet through the mountain. The three inversions, including a vertical loop and sidewinder, are perfectly paced, and the smooth transitions make for a thrilling ride.

Although the ride is relatively short, it's packed with high-energy moments that leave riders breathless. Some may experience slight discomfort due to the speed and intensity, and it is common to experience "grayouts" due to the G-forces. The coaster has a rugged charm, with theming around the station building adding to its appeal.

Admission (Ticket) ($):
- General admission to Dollywood is required for entry, with daily tickets starting at around $89 USD for adults.

Nearby Attractions:
- **Wild Eagle**: Another popular coaster in Dollywood, known for its smooth ride and unique seating design.
- **Dollywood's Splash Country**: A family-friendly water park located near the amusement park.

Important Information for Visitors:
Riders should be aware that the Tennessee Tornado can be intense, and those with back issues or other health concerns should proceed with caution. The coaster occasionally undergoes maintenance, so it's recommended to check availability during your visit.

Natchez Trace Parkway Bridge

Location:
Natchez Trace Pkwy, Franklin, TN 37064, United States
Plus Code:
X2P5+G5 Franklin, Tennessee, USA
Website: www.npplan.com
Contact: +1 800-305-7417
Opening Hours: Open 24 hours
Description:

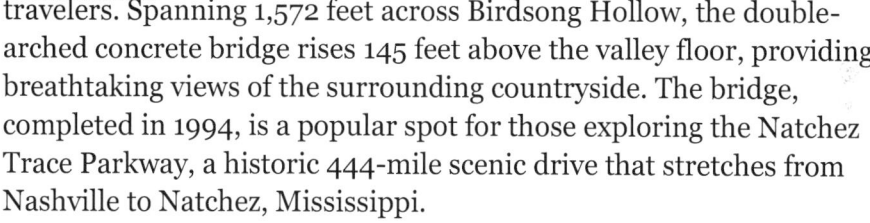

The Natchez Trace Parkway Bridge is an iconic architectural landmark located near Franklin, Tennessee, offering a scenic and serene experience for travelers. Spanning 1,572 feet across Birdsong Hollow, the double-arched concrete bridge rises 145 feet above the valley floor, providing breathtaking views of the surrounding countryside. The bridge, completed in 1994, is a popular spot for those exploring the Natchez Trace Parkway, a historic 444-mile scenic drive that stretches from Nashville to Natchez, Mississippi.

There is a pull-off area near the bridge where visitors can stop to take in the views, but amenities are limited to parking, making it more of a quick scenic stop than a full tourist destination. The Parkway itself offers a peaceful drive, free from trucks and heavy traffic, making it ideal for a relaxing day trip. Along the drive, visitors can enjoy wildlife sightings, historical markers, and picturesque waterfalls.

While the bridge is a marvel of engineering, it has also been the site of some tragic events. Efforts to improve safety, including the installation of barriers, have greatly reduced these incidents. Visitors are encouraged to enjoy the views responsibly and to seek help if they see anyone in distress.

Nearby Attractions:
- **Meriwether Lewis Memorial**: A historic site located along the Natchez Trace Parkway.
- **Franklin**: A nearby town with rich history, including Civil War landmarks and charming local shops.

Important Information for Visitors:
While the bridge offers stunning views, visitors should be aware that the area is primarily a scenic stop with no restrooms or other facilities. If

planning to explore the Parkway, bring essentials and enjoy the natural beauty at your own pace.

Carnton

Location: 1345 Eastern Flank Cir, Franklin, TN 37064, United States
Plus Code: W43R+7M Franklin, Tennessee, USA
Website: www.boft.org
Contact: +1 615-794-0903
Opening Hours:
- Monday to Saturday: 9 am – 5 pm
- Sunday: 10 am – 5 pm

Description: Carnton is a historic plantation in Franklin, Tennessee, deeply tied to the Battle of Franklin during the Civil War. The mansion served as a field hospital for Confederate soldiers, and the grounds are home to the McGavock Confederate Cemetery, where nearly 1,500 soldiers are buried. Today, Carnton offers an immersive look into its history through guided tours, which provide visitors with stories of the McGavock family, the soldiers, and the community during the war.

The site has been well-preserved, with carefully curated rooms showcasing artifacts and period furnishings, giving visitors a glimpse into 19th-century life. Highlights of the tour include the Confederate Cemetery, one of the oldest Osage Orange trees in Tennessee, and the family Bible. Tours are highly informative, with expert guides sharing vivid details about the Battle of Franklin and the significant role Carnton played in it.

Nearby Attractions:
- **Carter House**: Another historic home tied to the Battle of Franklin, often visited in conjunction with Carnton.
- **Downtown Franklin**: Offers a variety of shops, restaurants, and historical landmarks.

Admission (Ticket) ($):
Combination tickets with Carter House are available and recommended for a comprehensive experience.

Important Information for Visitors:
Reservations are recommended, especially during peak times. Be sure to wear comfortable walking shoes, as the tour includes both the mansion and the surrounding grounds.

The Escape Game Nashville (Opry Mills)

Location: 523 Opry Mills Dr, Nashville, TN 37214, United States
Located in: Opry Mills
Plus Code: 6844+57 Nashville, Tennessee, USA
Website:
www.theescapegame.com

Contact: +1 615-235-5742
Opening Hours:
- Monday to Sunday: 8 am – 12 am

Description:
The Escape Game Nashville, located within the Opry Mills shopping complex, offers an immersive escape room experience with highly interactive and intricately designed game rooms. The variety of puzzles and challenges caters to all ages, making it a perfect destination for families, friends, and groups. The rooms include complex themes like "Special Ops: The Market," known for its impressive visuals and interactive video elements, where actions trigger responses that enhance the game's atmosphere. The staff is praised for being welcoming and passionate, ensuring a smooth and fun experience for all participants.

Each escape room provides a different level of difficulty and storyline, giving returning players fresh challenges. The combination of mental challenges, teamwork, and immersive settings makes The Escape Game a standout attraction in Nashville.

Nearby Attractions:
- **Opry Mills**: A massive shopping complex with numerous stores, dining options, and entertainment.
- **Grand Ole Opry**: Just a short distance away, it offers tours and live music performances.

Admission (Ticket) ($):
Ticket prices vary depending on the specific game and time slot, typically starting at around $39.99 per person.
Important Information for Visitors:
Advanced booking is recommended to secure your preferred time slot. Rooms accommodate groups of varying sizes, and it's suggested to arrive early for briefing and orientation.

Discovery Center at Murfree Spring

Location: 502 SE Broad St, Murfreesboro, TN 37130, United States
Plus Code: RJQ7+G5 Murfreesboro, Tennessee, USA
Website:
www.explorethedc.org
Contact: +1 615-890-2300
Opening Hours:
- Monday: Closed
- Tuesday to Saturday: 10 am – 5 pm
- Sunday: 12 pm – 5 pm

Description:
The Discovery Center at Murfree Spring is a hands-on children's museum and nature center designed to inspire and educate young minds through interactive exhibits and outdoor exploration. This family-friendly destination features a wide range of engaging exhibits, from science and art to environmental education. Popular indoor activities include water play areas, where children can engage with water-based experiments, and a variety of interactive displays that cater to different age groups, including toddlers and older children.

The outdoor area is equally impressive, with a playground, a water exhibit, and a walking trail that connects to the Murfree Spring Wetlands, offering kids a chance to explore nature up close. The center is clean, spacious, and well-maintained, with accessible restrooms and a welcoming atmosphere created by friendly staff.

Admission (Ticket) ($):
- Adults: $10
- Children (2 and up): $8

Nearby Attractions:
- **Cannonsburgh Village**: A reconstructed pioneer village located nearby.
- **Oaklands Mansion**: A historic house and museum showcasing antebellum history in Murfreesboro.

Important Information for Visitors:
The center is highly recommended for families with children, especially for those looking for an educational yet fun day out. Most exhibits are in working order, but it's worth checking ahead for any temporary closures. The outdoor area is great for sunny days, while the indoor exhibits provide plenty of activities for colder or rainy days. No reservations are necessary.

Lotz House Museum

Location: 1111 Columbia Ave, Franklin, TN 37064, United States
Plus Code: W49G+4W Franklin, Tennessee, USA
Website: www.lotzhouse.com
Contact: +1 615-790-7190
Opening Hours:
- Monday to Saturday: 9 am – 5 pm
- Sunday: 11 am – 4 pm

Description: The Lotz House Museum, located in the heart of Franklin, Tennessee, offers an immersive glimpse into Civil War history through the lens of the Lotz family and their iconic home. The house played a significant role in the 1864 Battle of Franklin, and visitors can explore the carefully preserved rooms filled with original furnishings and artifacts. The museum stands out for allowing guests to physically enter the rooms rather than just viewing them from doorways, providing a deeper connection to history.

Knowledgeable guides, such as Chuck and Will, enrich the experience with detailed accounts of the Lotz family, Civil War stories, and fascinating local history. The museum also offers ghost tours for those interested in paranormal history. Visitors rave about the interactive nature of the tour, friendly staff, and the low cost of entry, making this an ideal destination for history enthusiasts and curious tourists alike.

Admission (Ticket) ($):
$12 per adult (converted to USD)

Nearby Attractions:
- **Carter House**: A historic home connected to the Battle of Franklin, located nearby.
- **Carnton**: Another significant Civil War site that complements the Lotz House visit.

Important Information for Visitors:
Reservations are recommended for busy weekends and special tours like ghost tours. The museum offers group rates and packages through sightseeing passes, adding value for multi-attraction visits in the Nashville and Franklin areas.

Earth Experience - Middle Tennessee Museum of Natura History

Location: 816 Old Salem Rd, Murfreesboro, TN 37129, United States
Plus Code: RHPW+PX Murfreesboro, Tennessee, USA
Website: www.earthexperience.org
Contact: +1 615-900-8358
Opening Hours:
- Wednesday to Saturday: 11 am – 4 pm
- Sunday to Tuesday: Closed

Description: The Earth Experience - Middle Tennessee Museum of Natural History is a hidden gem in Murfreesboro, offering a fascinating look into prehistoric life, geology, and the natural history of Tennessee. Although small in size, the museum is packed with authentic fossils, including a towering T-Rex skeleton, and exhibits that explore Tennessee's geology, caves, fossils, and minerals. Visitors can also learn about the origin of the Nashville Predators' saber-tooth tiger mascot and discover Tennessee's state rock and shell.

The museum features friendly, knowledgeable staff who enhance the experience with engaging stories about dinosaurs and the natural world. It's a perfect place for families, offering an informative yet fun experience for both children and adults. While the space is cozy, plans for expansion are in the works, and donations are welcome to support the museum's growth.

Admission (Ticket) ($): $7 per adult
Nearby Attractions:
- **Cannonsburgh Village**: A historic village with reconstructed pioneer-era buildings.
- **Stones River National Battlefield**: A significant Civil War site located a short drive away.

Important Information for Visitors:
The museum is currently small but expanding, and donations are encouraged to support the growth of its collections and facilities. The gift shop offers a variety of unique souvenirs related to natural history. Reservations are not typically required, and visitors can expect a relaxed, educational visit with no long wait times.

Wander Nashville

Location: 100 1st Ave S, Nashville, TN 37201, United States
Plus Code: 569C+PV Nashville, Tennessee, USA
Website: www.wandernashville.com
Contact: +1 205-892-6337

Opening Hours:
- Friday to Monday: 9 am – 5 pm
- Tuesday and Wednesday: Closed
- Thursday: 9 am – 5 pm

Description: Wander Nashville offers an exhilarating and informative e-bike tour experience through the vibrant city of Nashville. The tour provides a unique way to explore Music City, with the assistance of pedal-assist electric bikes, making it easy to handle even the occasional uphill stretches. Equipped with helmets that feature speakers for direct communication from your guide, you can enjoy a narrated journey full of local history, cultural tidbits, and restaurant recommendations.

The tours are designed for both first-time and repeat visitors to Nashville, offering a blend of scenic routes, historic sites, and insider tips on neighborhoods worth visiting. Led by knowledgeable and friendly guides like Cash and Don, safety is a priority, and the relaxed pace ensures that everyone stays together. Ideal for all levels of riders, the e-bike tour is an excellent way to see Nashville's highlights in just a few hours.

Admission (Ticket) ($): $120 for two people

Nearby Attractions:
- **Nashville Riverfront Park**: A beautiful green space along the Cumberland River.
- **Country Music Hall of Fame**: A must-see for country music fans, located within a short ride.

Important Information for Visitors:

This LGBTQ+ friendly tour is suitable for riders of all experience levels. Helmets with speakers are provided for easy communication, and safety is prioritized throughout the tour. It's a great way to see the city up close while also receiving restaurant and activity recommendations from knowledgeable local guides.

The Cross

Location: Tennessee Ave, Sewanee, TN 37375, United States
Plus Code: 53R7+R3 Sewanee, Tennessee, USA
Opening Hours: Open 24 hours

Description: The Cross, located in Sewanee, Tennessee, offers a stunning and serene spot for reflection, prayer, and outdoor exploration. Perched on a hill, this iconic landmark provides sweeping views of the Tennessee landscape, making it a favorite destination for both locals and visitors. The site is easily accessible and has no entry fee, making it a popular spot for weddings and quiet personal moments. Visitors can enjoy peaceful walks on the surrounding trails while taking in the breathtaking scenery. Whether you're seeking a spiritual retreat or simply a beautiful view, The Cross is an ideal destination for nature lovers and those seeking tranquility.

Admission (Ticket) ($): Free

Nearby Attractions:
- **University of the South (Sewanee)**: A historic university known for its beautiful campus and Gothic architecture.
- **Sewanee Natural Bridge**: A scenic spot for nature enthusiasts and hikers.

Important Information for Visitors:
No reservations are needed, and the site is open 24/7, making it a convenient stop at any time of day. Sunrise and sunset offer particularly spectacular views from The Cross.

Shelby Bottoms Nature Center & Greenway

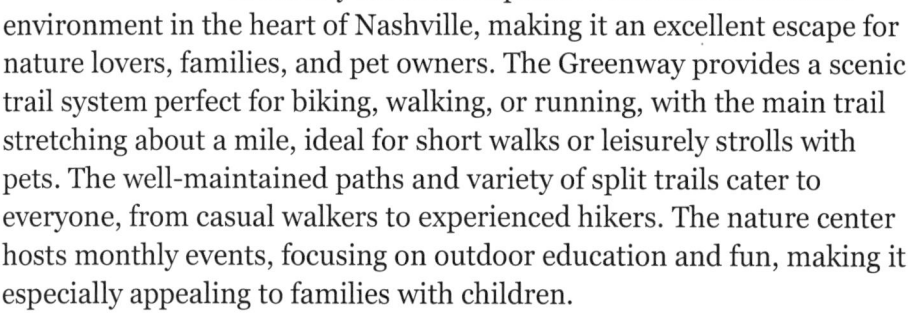

Location: 1900 Davidson St, Nashville, TN 37206, United States
Plus Code: 578G+C2 Nashville, Tennessee, USA
Opening Hours:
- Tuesday: 9 am – 4 pm
- Wednesday: 12 pm – 4 pm
- Thursday: 9 am – 4 pm
- Friday: 12 pm – 4 pm
- Saturday: 9 am – 4 pm
- Sunday & Monday: Closed

Website: https://www.nashville.gov
Contact: +1 615-862-8539
Description: Shelby Bottoms Nature Center & Greenway offers an expansive and diverse natural environment in the heart of Nashville, making it an excellent escape for nature lovers, families, and pet owners. The Greenway provides a scenic trail system perfect for biking, walking, or running, with the main trail stretching about a mile, ideal for short walks or leisurely strolls with pets. The well-maintained paths and variety of split trails cater to everyone, from casual walkers to experienced hikers. The nature center hosts monthly events, focusing on outdoor education and fun, making it especially appealing to families with children.

The surrounding greenery, serene river views, and abundant wildlife create a peaceful atmosphere, with plenty of opportunities to explore different routes and nature spots. There is also a dedicated nature play area for kids to enjoy. Whether you're a tourist or a local, the Shelby Bottoms Greenway provides a tranquil yet engaging outdoor experience.

Admission (Ticket) ($): Free
Nearby Attractions:
- **Shelby Park**: An expansive park with picnic areas, playgrounds, and fishing.
- **Cumberland River Greenway**: A nearby trail that runs alongside the river for extended outdoor adventures.

Important Information for Visitors:
The park is pet-friendly, offering a spacious area for pets and a safe playground for kids. The center is accessible for strollers and ideal for

family outings, providing various walking and hiking options suitable for all ages. The Greenway is open daily, but the nature center has specific operating hours.

Tennessee Agricultural Museum

Location: 404 Hogan Rd, Nashville, TN 37220, United States (Located in Ellington Agricultural Center)
Plus Code: 3763+XH Nashville, Tennessee, USA
Opening Hours:
- Monday to Friday: 9 am – 4 pm
- Saturday & Sunday: Closed

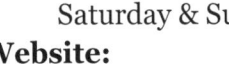

Website:
https://www.tnagmuseum.org
Contact: +1 615-837-5197

Description: The Tennessee Agricultural Museum, located within the Ellington Agricultural Center, offers a fascinating glimpse into the state's agricultural history. This free-to-enter museum operates on donations and showcases two floors filled with historic farming tools, machinery, and artifacts that illustrate Tennessee's rich agricultural past. Knowledgeable and passionate staff ensure an engaging visit, often bringing history to life with detailed stories about the exhibits.

Visitors will also find outdoor displays, adding to the museum's appeal. While the museum is off the beaten path, it remains a hidden gem for Middle Tennessee, with parking and restrooms available on-site. The museum also hosts community events such as Farm Day, making it a wonderful destination for both families and those interested in agricultural history.

Admission (Ticket) ($): Free (Donations appreciated)
Nearby Attractions:
- **Ellington Agricultural Center**: A large park featuring walking trails, gardens, and outdoor exhibits.
- **Nashville Zoo**: A short drive away for those looking to explore more of the area.

Important Information for Visitors:
Reservations are not required, and there is no wait time. The museum offers a calm, educational environment with friendly staff ready to answer questions. Parking and bathrooms are available, making it an accessible and convenient stop for visitors.

Tennessee Central Railway Museum

Location: 220 Willow St, Nashville, TN 37210, United States
Plus Code: 563W+X7 Nashville, Tennessee, USA
Opening Hours:
• Saturday: 10 am – 2 pm
• Closed on other days
Website: http://tcry.org
Contact: +1 615-244-9001
Description:
The Tennessee Central Railway Museum in Nashville offers a fascinating glimpse into the history of railroading, complete with educational exhibits and an opportunity to take scenic train excursions. The museum staff is known for their friendliness and hospitality, enhancing the experience with interactive performances, such as themed train robberies, which entertain passengers throughout the journey.

Popular excursions include wine-tasting trips to Watertown, where guests can enjoy a relaxing ride and sample local wines on board. Although Watertown has limited activities, the train ride itself, coupled with the scenic views and historical insight, makes it worth the trip. The museum also features model trains and exhibits that transport visitors back in time to the golden age of railroads.

Admission (Ticket) ($):
Tickets for train excursions vary based on the event and availability. Reservations are recommended for popular excursions, and prices are listed on the museum's website.

Nearby Attractions:
- **Nashville Zoo**: A short drive from the museum, perfect for a family outing.

- **Adventure Science Center**: An interactive museum offering fun for all ages.

Important Information for Visitors:
Reservations are highly recommended for the museum's train excursions, especially for special events like wine tours. The museum has a model train display, and guests can expect short wait times when visiting on weekends. Parking and restroom facilities are available on-site.

Fortress Rosecrans

Location: Golf Ln, Murfreesboro, TN 37129, United States
Plus Code: VH2Q+X6 Murfreesboro, Tennessee, USA
Website: https://www.nps.gov
Contact: +1 615-893-9501
Opening Hours:
Open daily, 24 hours
Description: Fortress Rosecrans, located in Murfreesboro, Tennessee, is one of the largest earthen fortifications built during the American Civil War. Constructed after the Battle of Stones River in 1863, it served as a vital Union supply depot, securing control of the area. Today, the remnants of the fort are preserved within a serene park setting, with paved trails winding through the historical mounds, offering visitors a peaceful walk through history.

Informational signs scattered throughout the site provide insight into the fort's role during the war and the significance of its construction. While some paths are well marked, others may lead to less clear areas, making it important for visitors to be mindful of their route. The trails offer views of nearby water, and the natural setting, with its cedar trees and bird calls, adds to the tranquil experience.

Admission (Ticket) ($): Free
Nearby Attractions:
- **Stones River National Battlefield**: Located nearby, this Civil War battlefield offers further exploration into the history of the area.

- **Murfreesboro Greenway System**: A network of trails for walking, biking, and exploring the natural beauty of the region.

Important Information for Visitors:
The site is open 24 hours, but it is recommended to visit during daylight to fully appreciate the historical markers and enjoy the scenic trails. No reservations are needed, and there are no entry fees. Be prepared for some unmarked paths that may lead to dead ends or unclear routes.

Fred Deadman Park

Location: Wilson St, Manchester, TN 37355, United States
Plus Code: FWP7+5F Manchester, Tennessee, USA
Website:
https://www.cityofmanchestertn.com
Contact: +1 931-728-0273
Opening Hours: Open 24 hours
Description: Fred Deadman Park in Manchester, Tennessee, is a family-friendly recreational space featuring a wide range of amenities for all ages. The park boasts multiple playgrounds, including accessible play areas designed for wheelchair users, and offers ample outdoor activities like tennis courts, baseball fields, a skate park, and a scenic walking trail. The paved walking path runs alongside a picturesque creek, dotted with benches and picnic tables, making it an ideal spot for relaxation or casual outdoor dining. Visitors can also enjoy a dedicated dog park, ensuring there's fun for the entire family, including pets.

Nearby Attractions:
- **Old Stone Fort State Archaeological Park:** A nearby historic site featuring ancient Native American ruins and additional hiking opportunities.

Important Information for Visitors:
The park is open 24/7, offering ample parking, clean facilities, and accessible features. It's a popular destination for families, dog owners, and outdoor enthusiasts.

Nelson's Green Brier Distillery

Location: 1414 Clinton St, Nashville, TN 37203, United States
Plus Code: 5672+CP Nashville, Tennessee, USA
Website: https://www.greenbrierdistillery.com
Contact: +1 615-913-8800
Opening Hours:
- Monday to Thursday: 11 am – 6 pm
- Friday to Saturday: 11 am – 7 pm
- Sunday: 10 am – 6 pm

Description: Nelson's Green Brier Distillery in Nashville is a must-visit destination for whiskey lovers and history buffs alike. Offering a variety of guided tours, the distillery provides an in-depth look at the whiskey-making process while sharing the rich history of the family-run business. The tour concludes with a tasting session, allowing guests to sample their premium spirits. Visitors can also enjoy a meal at the on-site restaurant, known for its generous portions and flavorful dishes, making it an excellent spot for lunch or a cocktail. The distillery's shop offers a range of whiskey bottles and branded merchandise, perfect for those wanting a memento of their visit.

Admission (Ticket):
Tours are typically ticketed, and reservations can be made via their website.

Nearby Attractions:
- **Marathon Village:** A historic automobile factory turned shopping and cultural destination.

Important Information for Visitors:
Reservations are recommended for tours, especially on weekends. There is ample parking available, and the venue is family-friendly.

Patsy Cline Museum

Location: 119 3rd Ave S, Nashville, TN 37201, United States (Located on the second floor above the Johnny Cash Museum)
Plus Code: 566F+9H Nashville, Tennessee, USA
Website: https://www.patsymuseum.com
Contact: +1 615-454-4722
Opening Hours:
- Monday to Sunday: 9 am – 7 pm

Description:
The Patsy Cline Museum, located in downtown Nashville, provides a comprehensive look into the life and career of one of country music's most iconic figures. This self-guided museum features memorabilia, personal items, and detailed exhibits that chronicle Patsy's rise to fame and the personal struggles that accompanied her short yet impactful career. Visitors can explore set-ups that recreate the decor of her Nashville home, offering a glimpse into her life beyond the stage. Whether you're a longtime fan or just learning about her, the museum's engaging displays bring Patsy Cline's legacy to life.

Admission (Ticket):
Tickets can be purchased at the door, with no wait time usually reported. Separate admission from the Johnny Cash Museum.

Nearby Attractions:
- **Johnny Cash Museum** (located in the same building)
- **Ryman Auditorium**
- **Country Music Hall of Fame**

Important Information for Visitors:
Reservations are not mandatory but recommended, especially during peak times. The museum is centrally located with food and drinks nearby for after your visit.

NashTrash Tours

Location: 900 Rosa L Parks Blvd, Nashville, TN 37208, United States (Located in Nashville Farmers' Market)
Plus Code: 5696+QM Nashville, Tennessee, USA
Website:
https://www.nashtrash.com
Contact: +1 615-226-7300
Opening Hours:
Open 24 hours (Check website for tour times)
Description: NashTrash Tours offers a uniquely hilarious and entertaining experience around Nashville, led by the dynamic Jugg Sisters. This irreverent comedy bus tour is a perfect way to explore the city with a twist, as it blends humor and local insights. The tour lasts a little over two hours and provides a highly interactive experience with personal shoutouts to passengers. Their comedic commentary keeps you so engaged that sightseeing becomes secondary to the fun and laughs. Suitable for adults and LGBTQ+ friendly, the tour is highly recommended for anyone looking for a light-hearted and memorable way to see Nashville. Be sure to reserve a spot, as this popular tour often fills up quickly.

Nearby Attractions:
- **Nashville Farmers' Market**
- **Bicentennial Capitol Mall State Park**
- **Tennessee State Museum**

Important Information for Visitors:
Reservations are highly recommended due to the tour's popularity. Consider arriving early to explore the Nashville Farmers' Market before boarding. Free parking is available in the overflow lot nearby.

John Seigenthaler Pedestrian Bridge

Location: Nashville, TN 37201, United States
Plus Code: 566G+GH Nashville, Tennessee, USA
Website:
https://www.nashville.gov
Opening Hours: Open 24 hours
Description: The John Seigenthaler Pedestrian Bridge spans the Cumberland River, offering stunning views of Nashville's skyline and the vibrant Music City.

This iconic bridge is a must-visit for its picturesque vistas, making it a popular spot for photography, especially at sunset and nighttime when the city lights up. It's an excellent location for a leisurely walk or a casual stroll, providing access to various nearby attractions. During the day, you might encounter street performers adding to the lively atmosphere. Although parking is limited, there are options for parallel parking near Nissan Stadium. Be mindful that some individuals may use the bridge as a place to sleep at night. The bridge is equipped with both elevators and stairs, making it accessible for all.

Nearby Attractions:
- **Nissan Stadium**
- **Music City Walk of Fame Park**
- **The Pedestrian Bridge's surrounding parks and riverside areas**

Important Information for Visitors:
The bridge is open 24 hours, providing flexibility for visits at any time of day. It's a popular spot, so visiting early in the morning or later in the evening may offer a more peaceful experience.

Geographic Center of Tennessee

Location: 307 Old Lascassas Rd, Murfreesboro, TN 37130, United States
Plus Code: VJ5Q+V5 Murfreesboro, Tennessee, USA
Website:
https://www.tnvacation.com
Opening Hours: Open 24 hours

Description: The Geographic Center of Tennessee is a modest yet notable landmark marking the central point of the state. Located just off Old Lascassas Road, this site offers a unique photo opportunity for visitors interested in Tennessee's geographical history. While the area is small and often overlooked, it provides a meaningful stop for those traveling through Murfreesboro. The site could benefit from further development and signage to enhance its visibility and appeal. Although currently lacking in extensive amenities, it is a free attraction and is close to Middle Tennessee State University. Visitors are encouraged to enjoy a brief visit and take a few photos. Please be mindful of the area's current condition, as some litter and minor maintenance issues have been reported.

Nearby Attractions:
- Middle Tennessee State University
- Murfreesboro's Historic Downtown Area

Important Information for Visitors:
The site is accessible at any time, making it convenient for quick stops. The area is generally clean but may have some litter, so bringing a small trash bag to keep the site tidy is appreciated. Parking is limited, so plan accordingly.

Steepest Pavement in Middle Tennessee

Location: Nashville, TN 37210, United States
Plus Code: 47R5+CR Nashville, Tennessee, USA
Opening Hours: Open 24 hours
Description: The Steepest Pavement in Middle Tennessee is a notable landmark known for its impressive incline. Situated in Nashville, this spot is a unique challenge for those looking to test their stamina. The steepness of the hill makes it a significant site for hiking enthusiasts and those interested in unusual geographical features. The climb is demanding and provides a rigorous workout, making it an intriguing destination for adventurous visitors. While the area itself is free to access, the physical

challenge it presents can be a memorable experience, particularly for those who enjoy pushing their limits. The steep pavement is not just a test of physical endurance but also a conversation piece for those exploring Nashville.

Nearby Attractions:
- **Marathon Village**
- **Nashville's Historic Downtown Area**

Important Information for Visitors:
The site is open at all hours, allowing for flexible visiting times. Visitors should be prepared for a strenuous climb and consider their physical condition before attempting the ascent. Parking is available in the nearby area, and while no reservations are needed, it's a good idea to check for any local advice or tips on tackling the climb. The experience is free, but the challenge it poses makes it a rewarding achievement for many.

Parrot Mountain and Gardens

Location: 1471 McCarter Hollow Rd, Pigeon Forge, TN 37862, United States

Plus Code: RF6J+MF Pigeon Forge, Tennessee, USA

Opening Hours:
- **Friday:** 10 am – 6 pm
- **Saturday:** 10 am – 6 pm
- **Sunday:** 10 am – 6 pm
- **Monday:** 10 am – 6 pm
- **Tuesday:** 10 am – 6 pm
- **Wednesday:** 10 am – 6 pm
- **Thursday:** 10 am – 6 pm

Website: parrotmountainandgardens.com

Contact: +1 865-774-1749

Description: Parrot Mountain and Gardens offers a unique and interactive experience for bird enthusiasts and families. The attraction features a diverse collection of over 800 birds, including many rare and colorful species. Visitors can enjoy feeding and handling the birds, with opportunities to take memorable photos in a well-maintained environment. The gardens provide a beautiful and serene backdrop, adding to the overall experience. A highlight for many is the "babies room," where guests can hold and interact with young parrots. The facility also includes a deli with a covered picnic area for dining.

Restrooms:
Clean and adequately sized restrooms are available on-site.

Picnic Area:
A deli offers food options, which can be enjoyed on a covered picnic deck.

Admission (Ticket) ($): $30 per adult (price subject to change)

Important Information for Visitors:
- The site is located on a steep hill, which may affect parking and accessibility.
- Steep inclines are present throughout the grounds, but resting spots and golf cart tours are available.
- Souvenirs and photos are available at higher prices, contributing to the maintenance of the facility and care of the birds.

Nearby Attractions:
- **Great Smoky Mountains National Park**
- **Dollywood Theme Park**

The Dolly Parton Experience

Location: 2700 Dollywood Parks Blvd, Pigeon Forge, TN 37863, United States

Plus Code: QFW7+3X Pigeon Forge, Tennessee, USA

Opening Hours:
- **Friday to Thursday:** 10 am – 10 pm

Website: dollywood.com

Description: The Dolly Parton Experience, located within Dollywood, is a new and must-see exhibit that showcases the life and legacy of the iconic country singer and entertainer, Dolly Parton. This interactive museum takes visitors through a journey of Dolly's early life in the Smoky Mountains, her global rise to fame, and highlights key moments from her career. Key attractions include a replica of her childhood home, a chance to explore her famous tour bus, and a dedicated glam exhibit showcasing her iconic outfits and wigs.

Guests can immerse themselves in her world through various interactive displays, including a 360-degree projection show about her life and a simulated recording studio where visitors can sing along to her hits. The exhibit is air-conditioned and takes around an hour to explore. Dolly's tour bus only allows a few visitors at a time, so there may be a brief wait outside in the sun.

Important Information for Visitors:
- The experience is family-friendly with interactive exhibits for children.
- Expect some wait time for the tour bus, but other areas generally have no lines.
- Consider visiting nearby attractions within Dollywood, such as Red's Drive-In for a meal after your tour.

Nearby Attractions:
- **Dollywood Theme Park**
- **Great Smoky Mountains National Park**

The Dolly Parton Experience is the perfect stop for fans of Dolly or anyone looking to learn more about country music history while visiting Dollywood.

Historic Travellers Rest Historic House Museum

Location: 636 Farrell Pkwy, Nashville, TN 37220, United States

Plus Code: 36GP+C7 Nashville, Tennessee, USA

Website: www.historictravellersrest.org

Contact: +1 615-832-8197

Opening Hours:
Friday to Saturday: 10am – 4:30pm
Sunday to Monday: Closed
Tuesday to Thursday: 10am – 4:30pm

Description: Historic Travellers Rest Historic House Museum offers a comprehensive look into Tennessee's past through its well-preserved estate. Visitors can explore the historical home where Andrew Jackson conducted business and experience a variety of historical exhibits. The site features a one-room schoolhouse and interactive activities, such as writing with quill pens, making it suitable for families and educational groups. The museum includes displays of Native American, African American, and American history, along with railroad history. The venue is also used for events, including weddings, providing picturesque settings and professional service.

Admission (Ticket) ($): Free
Nearby Attractions:
- Andrew Jackson's Hermitage (approximately 10 miles away)
- The Country Music Hall of Fame (approximately 13 miles away)

Important Information for Visitors:
It is recommended to visit during open hours, and reservations are not required. Parking is available on-site, but it is advisable to check current conditions and accessibility.

Downtown Lebanon

Location: Public Square, Lebanon, TN 37087, United States
Plus Code: 6P55+5H Lebanon, Tennessee, USA
Website: www.downtownlebanontn.com
Opening Hours: Downtown Lebanon does not have specific operating hours as it is an open area with various businesses operating at different times.
Description: Downtown Lebanon, situated in the heart of Lebanon, Tennessee, offers a glimpse into the town's historic charm. Visitors can explore a mix of quaint shops, local eateries, and offices housed in historic buildings. The downtown area features several notable establishments, including the guitar shop and Harper's Book Store, which stand out as popular spots. Despite its potential, the area faces challenges with several vacant storefronts and limited dining options, which may impact the overall visitor experience. While the downtown does have some historic appeal and friendly locals, it may not yet serve as a major tourist destination. A visit to Downtown Lebanon offers a peaceful, small-town experience

with opportunities to explore local history and shop at a few unique stores.
Admission (Ticket) ($): Free to visit; individual shops and restaurants may have their own pricing.
Nearby Attractions: While Downtown Lebanon itself may be limited in attractions, nearby points of interest include local parks and historical sites that can provide additional activities for visitors.
Important Information for Visitors: The area is generally open and accessible without specific hours, but individual businesses will have their own operating times. It is advisable to check with specific stores or eateries for their hours before visiting.

Pennington Cave

Location: Winchester, TN 37398, United States
Plus Code: 6PXF+9F Winchester, Tennessee, USA
Opening Hours: Open 24 hours
Description: Pennington Cave, located near Tim's Ford in Winchester, Tennessee, offers an intriguing adventure for outdoor enthusiasts. Accessible primarily by boat, the cave is a popular spot for those exploring the area's natural beauty. Visitors can experience the cave's depth, which extends several hundred feet and includes a rope-assisted climb to a higher level. The cave features various tight spaces and natural formations, making it a unique destination for spelunking. It's recommended to bring a flashlight for exploring and be prepared for a lively underwater environment with fish in the cave's waters. The surrounding area also includes a beautiful setting with opportunities for swimming and picnicking. The cave is part of a larger scenic experience that includes the Sunset Cruise at Tim's Ford, which provides views of the cave and nearby waterfall.
Admission (Ticket) ($): Free
Nearby Attractions: The nearby Tim's Ford Lake offers additional recreational opportunities, including boating, fishing, and hiking.

Important Information for Visitors: The cave is accessible via boat, and visitors should be prepared for variable water levels and potential tight spaces. It is advisable to bring a flashlight for safety and exploration. The cave's environment includes active wildlife, so be prepared for interactions with fish while swimming.

Nashville Looks Good On You Mural

Location: 2511 12th Ave S, Nashville, TN 37204, United States
Plus Code: 46F5+RV Nashville, Tennessee, USA
Website: www.nash.tn
Opening Hours: Open 24 hrs

Description: The "Nashville Looks Good On You" mural is a vibrant and charming photo spot located in the trendy 12 South neighborhood of Nashville. Tucked away behind The Frothy Monkey café in a parking lot, this mural provides a less crowded alternative to other popular murals in the area, such as "I Believe In Nashville." It serves as a fantastic backdrop for photos and selfies. Visitors can enjoy

exploring the surrounding 12 South area, known for its eclectic mix of shops, eateries, and scenic spots. The mural is easily accessible and adds a touch of local color to any visit to Nashville.
Admission (Ticket) ($): Free
Nearby Attractions: While visiting the mural, you can explore The Frothy Monkey for excellent coffee, and enjoy the vibrant 12 South neighborhood with its variety of shops and dining options.
Important Information for Visitors: The mural is located behind The Frothy Monkey, so GPS directions will guide you directly to it. There is no need for reservations or entry fees.

Taylor Swift Bench

Location: Centennial Park, Nashville, TN 37203, United States

Plus Code: 552P+85 Nashville, Tennessee, USA

Opening Hours: Open 24 hours (Monday to Sunday)

Description: The Taylor Swift Bench, located in Nashville's iconic Centennial Park, is a notable and relaxing spot for fans of the pop superstar. While the bench itself may seem ordinary, its connection to Taylor Swift and the beautiful surroundings of the park make it a popular destination for photos, peaceful reflection, and socializing. Situated under the shade of a willow tree, it offers a serene atmosphere amidst the hustle of the city. Visitors often take pictures, enjoy the view of the park, and engage in casual conversations with fellow fans. There's no wait or reservation needed to enjoy the bench, making it an easily accessible landmark in one of Nashville's most beloved parks.

Admission (Ticket) ($): Free

Nearby Attractions: Centennial Park offers many attractions, including the famous Parthenon, a full-scale replica of the ancient Greek temple, as well as beautiful walking paths, a pond, and open spaces for picnics or relaxation.

Important Information for Visitors: Though the bench itself may not have any special decorations, its location under a scenic willow tree in Centennial Park makes it a peaceful spot for Taylor Swift fans and casual visitors alike. No reservation is necessary, and the area is usually quiet and easy to access.

Rattle and Snap Plantation

Location: 1522 N Main St, Columbia, TN 38401, United States
Plus Code: HR6V+CG Columbia, Tennessee, USA
Website: www.rattleandsnapplantation.com
Contact: +1 931-379-1700

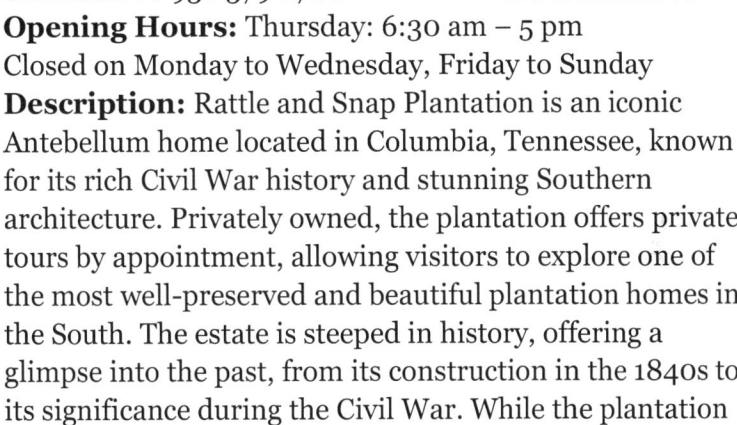

Opening Hours: Thursday: 6:30 am – 5 pm
Closed on Monday to Wednesday, Friday to Sunday
Description: Rattle and Snap Plantation is an iconic Antebellum home located in Columbia, Tennessee, known for its rich Civil War history and stunning Southern architecture. Privately owned, the plantation offers private tours by appointment, allowing visitors to explore one of the most well-preserved and beautiful plantation homes in the South. The estate is steeped in history, offering a glimpse into the past, from its construction in the 1840s to its significance during the Civil War. While the plantation is not open for regular hours, the detailed private tours offer an intimate and educational experience, providing deep insight into the life and times of the South during the Antebellum period. For those interested in architecture, Southern history, or Civil War heritage, this plantation is a hidden gem worth visiting.
Admission (Ticket) ($): Private tours only (contact for details)
Nearby Attractions: Columbia offers a number of nearby historic attractions, including the James K. Polk Home and Museum, and downtown Columbia, known for its charming Southern ambiance.
Important Information for Visitors: Tours must be scheduled in advance, and no walk-ins are accepted. Highly recommended to contact ahead for availability, as this is a privately owned estate.

Natchez Trace Parkway Sign

Location: Franklin, TN 37064, United States
Plus Code: 225C+3P Franklin, Tennessee, USA
Opening Hours: Open 24 hours
Description: The Natchez Trace Parkway is a 500-mile scenic drive steeped in history, stretching from Natchez, Mississippi, to Nashville, Tennessee. The parkway sign in Franklin, TN, marks the entrance to one of America's most beloved routes, free from commercial vehicles and designed for leisurely travel. With a speed limit of 50 mph, the drive offers a relaxing escape with stunning views, especially during the fall when the foliage is at its peak. Along the parkway, there are numerous historical stops, scenic overlooks, and opportunities for hiking and exploring. The sign is a popular spot for photos before beginning the journey. Whether you are on a quick stop for a picture or embarking on a longer road trip, the Natchez Trace Parkway offers a peaceful and scenic way to experience nature and history.

Admission (Ticket) ($): Free
Nearby Attractions: In Franklin, TN, visitors can also explore historic downtown Franklin, Carnton House, and the Carter House, all offering glimpses into Tennessee's Civil War past.
Important Information for Visitors: No reservation is required. The parkway is ideal for a leisurely drive with numerous pull-off points to explore the surrounding natural beauty and historical sites.

Rowing Man Statue

Location: W. Church Avenue & S Gay St, Knoxville, TN 37902, United States
Plus Code: X37J+9X Knoxville, Tennessee, USA
Opening Hours: Open 24 hours

Tennessee Explorer's Bucket List

Description: The Rowing Man Statue, located at Two Centre Square in downtown Knoxville, is a unique piece of public art. The statue is a  symbol of perseverance, representing Knoxville's ability to overcome adversity, much like the figure who rows out of the depths. Many believe the statue depicts Suttree, the main character from Cormac McCarthy's novel *Suttree*, which is set in Knoxville. This corner of downtown provides ample space to relax and take in the surrounding cityscape. The statue isn't necessarily a destination but is a delightful surprise for those exploring the area, making it a popular spot for photos and a casual rest during a downtown walk.

Admission (Ticket) ($): Free

Nearby Attractions: Situated in the heart of Knoxville, visitors can explore other nearby attractions, including Market Square, the Tennessee Theatre, and the Knoxville Museum of Art.

Important Information for Visitors: No reservation is required, and the statue is easily accessible at any time, making it an ideal stop for those exploring downtown Knoxville.

I Believe In Nashville Mural

Location: 2702 12th Ave S, Nashville, TN 37204, United States

Plus Code: 46F6+63 Nashville, Tennessee, USA

Website: www.ibelieveinnashville.com

Opening Hours: Open 24 hours

Description: The *I Believe In Nashville* mural is one of the most  iconic public art installations in Nashville, located in the vibrant 12 South neighborhood. This mural, with its patriotic red, white, and blue design, has become a must-visit photo opportunity for tourists and locals alike. Set against the backdrop of boutique shops, restaurants, and coffee houses, the mural serves as a symbol of local pride and resilience. Parking is available in a nearby lot, but visitors often park briefly in the alley for a quick photo op. Early morning visits are recommended to avoid crowds, especially on weekends. The mural is

well-maintained and located near popular spots like Edley's BBQ and Draper James, adding to its appeal as part of the 12 South walking experience.
Admission (Ticket) ($): Free
Nearby Attractions: 12 South is home to several other murals, along with boutique shopping, restaurants, and cafés like the famous Frothy Monkey and Five Daughters Bakery. Visitors can explore the neighborhood's trendy offerings and enjoy a relaxed, art-filled day.
Important Information for Visitors: No reservation is needed to visit the mural. Parking options include nearby lots, though free parking can be limited. Early morning or weekday visits are recommended to beat the crowds.

Taylor Swift Willow Tree

Location: 2530 Park Plaza, Nashville, TN 37203, United States (Centennial Park)
Plus Code: 552P+72 Nashville, Tennessee, USA
Opening Hours: Open 24 hours
Description: The Taylor Swift Willow Tree, located in the heart of  Nashville's Centennial Park, holds a special place for fans and visitors alike. Planted in May 2023, the tree has quickly become a unique symbol in the park. Though relatively small, the willow is a notable spot for its serene beauty and connection to Taylor Swift's legacy. Visitors often pair a visit here with a stop at the nearby Taylor Swift bench, making it a popular destination for those looking to take pictures and soak in the ambiance of Centennial Park. The tree's modest size contrasts with its emotional impact, as it has become a place of reflection and admiration for many, often leaving a lasting impression.
Admission (Ticket) ($): Free
Nearby Attractions: Centennial Park is home to a variety of other landmarks, including the iconic Parthenon replica and the Taylor Swift bench. Visitors can also enjoy the park's walking trails, gardens, and the picturesque Lake Watauga.

Important Information for Visitors: The Taylor Swift Willow Tree is located in an open public space, easily accessible at any time. No reservations are required, but early mornings or weekdays provide the best opportunities for peaceful visits.

Bigfoot Adventure TN Zipline

Location: 514 Brawley Rd, Tracy City, TN 37387, United States
Plus Code: 863H+8J Tracy City, Tennessee, USA
Website: bigfootadventuretn.com
Contact: +1 423-994-0280
Opening Hours:
- Monday to Saturday: 9 am–5 pm
- Sunday: 10 am–5 pm

Description: Bigfoot Adventure TN Zipline offers an exciting experience for thrill-seekers in a scenic natural setting. Situated in Tracy City, Tennessee, this zipline tour takes you soaring through beautiful landscapes, with some lines even crossing over water, providing a unique perspective of the area's stunning environment. The staff at Bigfoot Adventure are known for their friendliness and professionalism, with guides who help ensure that visitors feel safe and entertained throughout their journey. Whether you're an experienced adventurer or trying a zipline for the first time, the team will guide you with encouragement and humor, making this a memorable outing for families, friends, or solo travelers.

Nearby Attractions: Baggenstoss Farms, The Point overlook, and other outdoor activities available in Tracy City make it a great spot for those looking to camp or explore more of Tennessee's natural beauty.

Important Information for Visitors: Reservations are recommended, especially during peak times, and visitors should prepare for a variety of zip lines, each offering a different experience.

Historic Tours of Nashville

Location: 217B 6th Ave N, Nashville, TN 37219, United States
Plus Code: 5679+65 Nashville, Tennessee, USA
Website: nashvillehistoryontour.com
Contact: +1 615-838-4507
Opening Hours:
- Monday to Saturday: 8 am–8 pm
- Sunday: 8 am–1 am

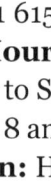

Description: Historic Tours of Nashville offers an immersive and engaging way to explore the city's rich past. Led by David Ewing, a knowledgeable and passionate guide with deep personal and familial ties to Nashville's history, these tours bring the city's pivotal moments to life. Ewing's tours focus on a variety of themes, including the Civil Rights Movement, women's suffrage, and the city's architectural evolution. Whether you're a visitor or local, the personalized nature of each tour ensures an enriching experience tailored to specific interests, from philanthropic efforts to education and activism. His firsthand storytelling, based on over 200 years of his family's history in the city, provides an in-depth and unique perspective on Nashville's transformative moments.
Nearby Attractions: Downtown Nashville, Ryman Auditorium, Tennessee State Capitol, and other iconic landmarks are easily accessible from the tour's starting location.
Important Information for Visitors: Tours are available for small and large groups, and reservations are recommended.

Shy's Hill

Location: Benton Smith Rd, Nashville, TN 37215, United States
Plus Code: 35QR+75 Nashville, Tennessee, USA
Website: bonps.org
Contact: +1 615-405-9000

Opening Hours:

- Monday to Sunday: 7 am–7 pm

Description: Shy's Hill is a historically significant site in Nashville, Tennessee, known for its role in the Battle of Nashville during the American Civil War. The site offers a winding, steep gravel path leading to the top, where visitors can explore interpretive boards providing historical information. At the summit, three flagpoles display weather-beaten flags representing the Confederate Army of Tennessee, the Union Army of Minnesota, and the U.S. flag. Although the area may lack some maintenance and additional features, it provides a peaceful and reflective environment for visitors interested in Civil War history. The hill is a quiet spot for contemplation and offers a panoramic view of Nashville. It's a free attraction, ideal for history enthusiasts and those seeking a tranquil setting.

Admission (Ticket) ($): Free

Nearby Attractions: Battle of Nashville Monument, Fort Negley Park, Tennessee State Museum

Important Information for Visitors: Wear sturdy shoes for the hike up the hill. The site is clean and well-kept, likely due to the surrounding neighborhood. It is recommended to visit during daylight hours, as the site is closed after dusk.

Buffalo Statues

Location: 610 Dickerson Pike, Nashville, TN 37207, United States

Plus Code: 56JG+MF Nashville, Tennessee, USA

Description: The Buffalo Statues on Dickerson Pike in Nashville are an eye-catching and unique landmark. These statues, located in a prominent area, offer an interesting visual element to the neighborhood. While their historical significance is not widely known, they stand as a notable feature in the local landscape. The statues would benefit from better maintenance and the addition of native plants to enhance their presentation. Currently, there are no dedicated parking spaces nearby, and additional crosswalks and public transportation options

would improve accessibility for visitors wanting to view the statues up close.
Admission (Ticket) ($): Free
Nearby Attractions: Shelby Park, Nashville Zoo at Grassmere, The Hermitage
Important Information for Visitors: Due to the lack of nearby parking, visitors may need to find street parking and walk to the statues. Improved accessibility features would make this attraction more convenient for those wishing to explore it further.

What Lifts You - West Nashville Mural

Location: 1114 Pine St, Nashville, TN 37203, United States
Plus Code: 5638+HC Nashville, Tennessee, USA
Opening Hours: Open 24 hours
Description: The "What Lifts You" mural, featuring iconic wings, is a popular photo spot in West Nashville. Known for its vibrant and artistic design, this mural provides a fantastic backdrop for memorable photos. It's considered one of the best of its kind, even when compared to murals in São Paulo or Florida. While it's somewhat hidden and easy to miss, the experience is rewarding with no significant wait times, especially if visited early in the morning. There is a trunk nearby to sit on, adding a unique touch to the photo opportunity.
Admission (Ticket) ($): Free
Nearby Attractions: Centennial Park, The Parthenon, Music Row
Important Information for Visitors: To avoid potential lines and crowds, visiting early in the day is recommended. While the mural is accessible at all times, parking might be limited, so plan accordingly.

Walter Hill Hydroelectric Station

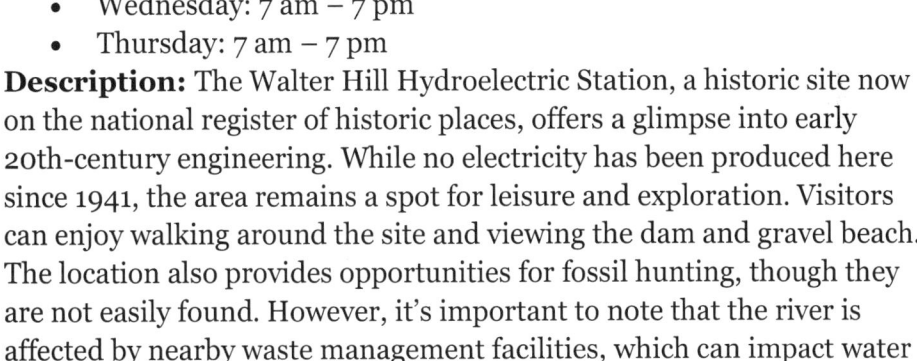

Location: Murfreesboro, TN 37130, United States
Plus Code: WJVF+35 Murfreesboro, Tennessee, USA
Website: murfreesborotn.gov
Opening Hours:
- Friday: 7 am – 7 pm
- Saturday: 7 am – 7 pm
- Sunday: 7 am – 7 pm
- Monday: 7 am – 7 pm
- Tuesday: 7 am – 7 pm
- Wednesday: 7 am – 7 pm
- Thursday: 7 am – 7 pm

Description: The Walter Hill Hydroelectric Station, a historic site now on the national register of historic places, offers a glimpse into early 20th-century engineering. While no electricity has been produced here since 1941, the area remains a spot for leisure and exploration. Visitors can enjoy walking around the site and viewing the dam and gravel beach. The location also provides opportunities for fossil hunting, though they are not easily found. However, it's important to note that the river is affected by nearby waste management facilities, which can impact water quality and odor. Swimming and consuming fish from this area are not recommended due to potential pollution.

Admission (Ticket) ($): Free

Nearby Attractions: Stones River National Battlefield, Cannonsburgh Village

Important Information for Visitors: Be aware of the potential for unpleasant odors from the nearby waste facilities, especially when the wind is blowing in the wrong direction. The site is a good spot for a casual visit and exploration, but visitors should avoid swimming or eating fish from the river.

Delta Riverboats

Location: 2800 Opryland Dr, Nashville, TN 37214, United States

Plus Code: 6864+C2 Nashville, Tennessee, USA

Website: gaylordopryland.com

Opening Hours:
- Friday: 10 am – 8 pm
- Saturday: 10 am – 8 pm
- Sunday: 10 am – 8 pm
- Monday: 10 am – 8 pm
- Tuesday: 10 am – 8 pm
- Wednesday: 10 am – 8 pm
- Thursday: 10 am – 8 pm

Description: The Delta Riverboats offer a scenic and relaxing boat ride through the lush interior of the Gaylord Opryland Resort & Convention Center. Located on the third floor of the resort, the ride provides a unique perspective on the hotel's indoor gardens and waterways. Guests can enjoy a humorous and informative tour led by knowledgeable guides, who share stories about the resort's history and features. The boat ride is suitable for all ages and provides a peaceful break from the busy resort environment. Due to its location within the resort, parking is available at Opry Mills Outlet Mall, as hotel parking can be expensive.

Admission (Ticket) ($): $11–15

Nearby Attractions: Gaylord Opryland Resort, Opry Mills Outlet Mall, Grand Ole Opry

Important Information for Visitors: The boat ride does not require reservations and tickets can be purchased on-site. Be aware that finding the boarding area may be confusing; asking an employee for directions or using a map can help. Expect a wait time of up to 30 minutes during peak times.

Old Town Trolley Tours Nashville

Location: 201 Broadway, Nashville, TN 37201, United States
Plus Code: 566F+MW Nashville, Tennessee, USA
Website: trolleytours.com
Contact: +1 629-208-0200
Opening Hours: 9 am – 4 pm Daily.
Description: Old Town Trolley Tours offers a comprehensive hop-on, hop-off tour of Nashville with 13 stops at key attractions around the city. This tour provides a great overview of Nashville's highlights, including the Country Music Hall of Fame, the American Pickers store, Jack Daniel's Distillery, and Music Row. The open-air trolleys feature high stadium seating for a clear view of the cityscape. The tour is guided by knowledgeable drivers who share insightful commentary about Nashville's history and landmarks. Although there may be some wait times at stops, the tour is well-organized and provides a thorough exploration of downtown neighborhoods and major attractions. Note that during adverse weather conditions, plastic windows may impair visibility.
Admission (Ticket) ($): Prices vary; typically around $35–45 for adults
Nearby Attractions: Country Music Hall of Fame, Jack Daniel's Distillery, American Pickers Store, Broadway, Capitol View
Important Information for Visitors: Reservations are recommended, especially during peak tourist seasons. The tour operates on a set schedule with a 2:00 pm cut-off, so plan accordingly to explore museums and other sites before returning to the trolley. The tour is a good option for those who want to get an overview of the city without the hassle of parking.

The Elephant Sanctuary in Tennessee — Elephant Discovery Center

Location: 27 E Main St, Hohenwald, TN 38462, United States
Plus Code: GCXX+7C Hohenwald, Tennessee, USA
Website: elephants.com
Contact: +1 931-796-6500
Opening Hours:
- Friday: 9 am – 4 pm
- Saturday: 9 am – 4 pm
- Sunday: Closed
- Monday: Closed
- Tuesday: 9 am – 4 pm
- Wednesday: 9 am – 4 pm
- Thursday: 9 am – 4 pm

Description: The Elephant Discovery Center provides an educational experience focused on the well-being and care of retired elephants. Visitors can watch live feeds of the elephants through the elecam, participate in interactive learning activities, and explore various informative displays about these majestic creatures. The center offers a unique opportunity to learn about the sanctuary's efforts to provide a peaceful and supportive environment for elephants retired from zoos and circuses. The staff is knowledgeable and helpful, enhancing the educational experience. Although the center is modest in terms of furnishings, its focus on the elephants' welfare is evident. Souvenirs and merchandise are available for purchase, and donations are encouraged to support the sanctuary's mission.

Admission (Ticket) ($): Prices not specified; usually free or by donation

Nearby Attractions: Hohenwald area has limited attractions; consider local shops or exploring the scenic countryside.

Important Information for Visitors: The center is closed on Sundays and Mondays, so plan your visit accordingly. The focus is on educational and interactive experiences rather than high-end amenities. Donations are welcomed to support the sanctuary's work.

"Musica" Statue

Location: Roundabout Plaza, 1600 Division St, Nashville, TN 37203, United States
Plus Code: 5625+R8 Nashville, Tennessee, USA
Website: alanlequire.com
Opening Hours: Open 24 hours
Description: The "Musica" statue is a striking public art installation located in the Roundabout Plaza of Music Row. Created by artist Alan LeQuire, this sculpture features a group of larger-than-life, abstractly nude figures in dynamic poses, celebrating the spirit of music and performance. Situated in a traffic roundabout, it serves as a prominent and accessible piece of art in Nashville. The statue's creative design and the use of figures symbolize the artistic energy and history of Music Row. The area around the statue is pedestrian-friendly, making it an easy stop for a quick visit or photo opportunity. Although the statue may be viewed as a "drive-by" attraction due to its location, it holds significant artistic value and contributes to the cultural landscape of Nashville.
Admission (Ticket) ($): Free
Nearby Attractions: Music Row, famous for its recording studios and historical significance in the music industry. Consider exploring nearby areas on foot or by scooter to fully appreciate the local history and culture.
Important Information for Visitors: The statue is accessible at any time as it is located in a public roundabout. No reservations are needed, and there is no wait time.

Belmont Mansion

Location: Belmont Blvd. and Acklen Ave, Nashville, TN 37212, United States
Plus Code: 46P4+63 Nashville, Tennessee, USA
Website: www.belmontmansion.com
Contact: +1 615-460-5459
Opening Hours:
Monday to Friday: 10 am – 3:30 pm
Saturday: 10 am – 3:30 pm
Sunday: 11 am – 3:30 pm
Admission (Ticket):
Guided Tour: $22 USD
Self-Guided Tour: $18 USD
Description: Belmont Mansion, located within Belmont University, is one of the most well-preserved antebellum homes in Nashville. It offers a deep dive into the history of the 19th century, showcasing unique architectural design and elegant furnishings from the period. Visitors can choose between a self-guided tour or a guided tour that provides a wealth of historical context about the mansion and its original owners. The guided tour, led by knowledgeable docents, covers the house's involvement in the Civil War era and its transition over time.

The mansion's interior is adorned with period-specific decor, which enhances the experience of stepping back into history. While the mansion holds significance in its association with both the grandeur and the darker history of the antebellum South, the docents ensure that a balanced and honest narrative is provided. The surrounding gardens offer a peaceful retreat, ideal for relaxing before or after the tour. Belmont Mansion is a must-see for history enthusiasts and anyone interested in Nashville's heritage. The mansion also features a quaint gift shop that offers replicas of period items, making it a great place for souvenirs.

Nearby Attractions:
- **Vanderbilt University**: A prestigious campus located just a short drive away.
- **Centennial Park**: Home to a replica of the Parthenon, this park is ideal for outdoor activities and sightseeing.

Important Information for Visitors:
- While reservations are not required, they are recommended, especially during peak tourist seasons.
- The mansion allows both self-guided and docent-led tours simultaneously, which can lead to some crowding.
- Parking is available on-site, and there is no time limit for visits during operating hours.
- Be sure to ring the doorbell upon arrival to gain entry to the mansion.

Miller Gap Overlook

Location: Miller Rd, Winchester, TN 37398, United States
Plus Code: 4V3F+MM Winchester, Tennessee, USA
Opening Hours: Open 24 hours daily
Description: Miller Gap Overlook, situated near Winchester, Tennessee, offers panoramic views of the surrounding valley. It is a scenic spot for those seeking a quiet and beautiful retreat into nature. The gravel road leading to the overlook can be challenging for vehicles, particularly low-clearance cars and street motorcycles, due to the uneven terrain, large rocks, and ruts. Visitors are highly advised to take Iron Gap Road to access Miller Road, as this is the safer route compared to TN-16.

While the view from the overlook is praised for its beauty, some visitors have noted that graffiti detracts from the natural environment. Still, the serene atmosphere and stunning vistas make it a worthwhile destination, particularly for those traveling in appropriate vehicles such as dual-sport motorcycles or high-clearance cars.

Important Information for Visitors:
- Exercise caution when driving to the overlook, especially if your vehicle has low clearance.
- If possible, avoid the direct route from TN-16 to Miller Road due to hazardous terrain and opt for Iron Gap Road instead.

- Be prepared for rough roads and ensure your vehicle is equipped for off-road conditions.

Nearby Attractions:
- **Tims Ford State Park**: Located nearby, this park offers hiking, boating, and other outdoor activities on Tims Ford Lake.
- **Winchester City Park**: A peaceful park within Winchester, perfect for picnics and family outings.

Hotels

Best Western Franklin Inn

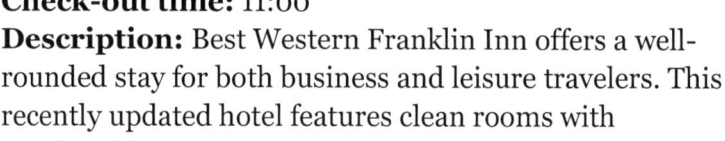

Location: 1308 Murfreesboro Rd, Franklin, TN 37064, United States
Plus Code: W57C+HV Franklin, Tennessee, USA
Contact: +1 615-790-0570
Website: www.bestwestern.com
Check-in time: 15:00
Check-out time: 11:00
Description: Best Western Franklin Inn offers a well-rounded stay for both business and leisure travelers. This recently updated hotel features clean rooms with comfortable beds and amenities that cater to a variety of needs. The property boasts ample parking space, suitable for vehicles with trailers. Guests appreciate the quiet atmosphere despite its proximity to major highways, making it a convenient stop for those looking to avoid heavy traffic. The hotel also offers a complimentary breakfast with diverse options, including a pancake machine, cereals, and hot foods. A playground and an outdoor pool make it family-friendly, while on-site laundry services are available for added convenience. Nearby, guests can find restaurants and grocery stores, further enhancing the ease of stay. With affordable pricing, this hotel offers an economical alternative to the higher prices of Nashville, without sacrificing quality or comfort.

Nearby Attractions: Shopping centers, I-65 highway, and dining options within close proximity.

Knights Inn Nashville

Location: 99 Spring St, Nashville, TN 37207, United States
Plus Code: 56GF+JP Nashville, Tennessee, USA
Contact: +1 615-678-6526
Website: www.knightsinn.com
Check-in time: 15:30
Check-out time: 23:00

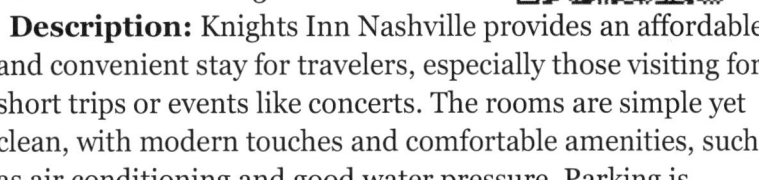

Description: Knights Inn Nashville provides an affordable and convenient stay for travelers, especially those visiting for short trips or events like concerts. The rooms are simple yet clean, with modern touches and comfortable amenities, such as air conditioning and good water pressure. Parking is available for a $10 fee, though this may be waived under certain circumstances. The hotel serves a complimentary breakfast with a variety of options, although some issues with the juice quality have been noted. Guests appreciate the friendly front desk service and the ease of check-in, though there have been isolated concerns about inconsistent treatment. The property is conveniently located near Nissan Stadium, allowing for easy walking access to events, and is close to major highways, making it ideal for road-trippers. Overall, this hotel offers value for its price, especially given its proximity to central Nashville.
Nearby Attractions: Nissan Stadium, downtown Nashville, restaurants, and shopping centers.

Hampton Inn McMinnville

Location: 1560 Sparta St, McMinnville, TN 37110, United States
Plus Code: M7X5+9P McMinnville, Tennessee, USA
Contact: +1 931-473-0009
Website: www.hilton.com
Check-in time: 15:00
Check-out time: 12:00

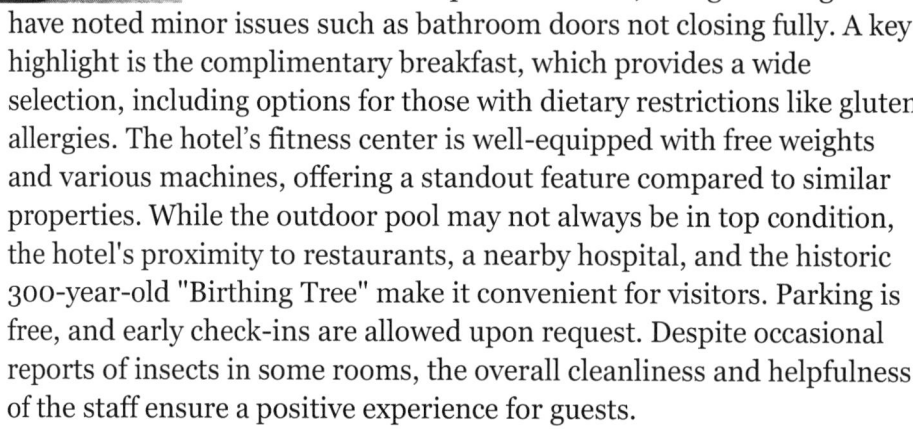

Description: Hampton Inn McMinnville offers a comfortable and modern stay with a variety of amenities suited for both leisure and business travelers. The hotel features clean and spacious rooms, though some guests have noted minor issues such as bathroom doors not closing fully. A key highlight is the complimentary breakfast, which provides a wide selection, including options for those with dietary restrictions like gluten allergies. The hotel's fitness center is well-equipped with free weights and various machines, offering a standout feature compared to similar properties. While the outdoor pool may not always be in top condition, the hotel's proximity to restaurants, a nearby hospital, and the historic 300-year-old "Birthing Tree" make it convenient for visitors. Parking is free, and early check-ins are allowed upon request. Despite occasional reports of insects in some rooms, the overall cleanliness and helpfulness of the staff ensure a positive experience for guests.
Nearby Attractions: The Three Star Mall, restaurants, and the historic Birthing Tree, all within walking distance.

Country Inn & Suites by Radisson, Nashville Airport East, TN

Location: 3423 Percy Priest Dr, Nashville, TN 37214, United States
Plus Code: 592C+WH Nashville, Tennessee, USA
Contact: +1 615-277-1099
Website: www.choicehotels.com

Check-in time: 15:00
Check-out time: 12:00
Description: Country Inn & Suites by Radisson, Nashville Airport East, offers affordable accommodation with a convenient location near Nashville's main attractions. The hotel features comfortable beds, simple but functional bathrooms, and a quiet environment for restful stays. Guests can enjoy a complimentary breakfast, which includes options like scrambled eggs, biscuits, and waffles. The hotel is ideal for travelers seeking value for money, though some have reported issues with cleanliness and maintenance, such as minor bugs and incomplete remodeling work. Despite these concerns, the friendly staff, including helpful front desk service, contribute to an overall positive experience. However, parking restrictions, particularly for vehicles with trailers, have been noted as a significant inconvenience for some guests, making it less suitable for those traveling with larger vehicles. The hotel's close proximity to downtown Nashville and various restaurants makes it a convenient option for exploring the city.
Nearby Attractions: Downtown Nashville, local restaurants, and shopping areas.

Best Western Heritage Inn

Location: 7641 Lee Hwy, Chattanooga, TN 37421, United States
Plus Code: 3V67+6X Chattanooga, Tennessee, USA
Contact: +1 423-899-3311
Website: www.bestwestern.com
Check-in time: 16:00
Check-out time: 11:00
Description: Best Western Heritage Inn in Chattanooga is a budget-friendly accommodation with easy access from I-75, ideal for travelers passing through. The hotel features clean and quiet rooms, though it is an older property with exterior doors and dated furnishings. While some rooms may show signs of wear, like chipped furniture and minor cleanliness issues, the staff is known for

their friendly and helpful service. Guests appreciate the comfortable beds, hot showers, and the convenience of accessing rooms directly from the parking area. The attached **City Cafe Diner** is a highlight, offering an extensive menu and excellent desserts. Although the hotel does not offer free breakfast, guests receive a 10% discount at the diner by showing their room key. The hotel has a pool, which is clean and inviting, though some minor room maintenance issues have been noted. Overall, it's a great value for the price, especially for short stays or those on a budget.

Nearby Attractions: Located conveniently near I-75, offering easy access to nearby Chattanooga attractions.

Wingate by Wyndham Goodlettsville

Location: 202 Northgate Cir, Goodlettsville, TN 37072, United States
Plus code: 88F2+H2 Goodlettsville, Tennessee, USA
Contact: +1 615-851-2828
Website: www.wyndhamhotels.com
Check-in time: 15:00
Check-out time: 11:00

Description: Wingate by Wyndham Goodlettsville offers a comfortable and accessible stay for both business and leisure travelers. Guests can enjoy clean, quiet rooms with modern amenities like Dove bath products, spacious bathrooms, and comfortable mattresses. The hotel is conveniently located within walking distance of numerous restaurants and a grocery store, making it easy to find dining options nearby. Families appreciate the kid-friendly atmosphere, while business travelers find the quiet environment ideal for working or relaxing. The outdoor pool offers a pleasant retreat, though some guests have suggested adding umbrellas to provide more shade.

The hotel's accessible rooms are spacious, though feedback indicates that improvements could be made to the bathroom facilities, such as adding grab bars and a more accessible bathtub. Guests also enjoy the breakfast, which offers a variety of options to start the day. However, some past

guests have expressed dissatisfaction with customer service experiences, particularly related to booking discrepancies and interactions with staff.
Nearby Attractions: Guests can explore the nearby historic Mansker's Station or enjoy local dining and shopping in Goodlettsville.

Super 8 by Wyndham Lakeland

Location: 9779 Huff N Puff Rd, Lakeland, TN 38002, United States
Plus code: 67F7+WH Lakeland, Tennessee, USA
Contact: +1 901-372-4575
Website: www.wyndhamhotels.com
Check-in time: 14:00
Check-out time: 11:00

Description: Super 8 by Wyndham Lakeland offers a budget-friendly stay with convenient access to Lakeland and nearby Memphis. The motel is suitable for travelers looking for basic accommodation and provides clean rooms that meet the needs of guests. The outdoor pool is an appreciated feature, though some guests have reported inconsistent availability. The motel's location, away from the busy Memphis area, ensures a quieter environment.

While the motel serves as an affordable option for many travelers, especially those on business trips or passing through, there have been mixed experiences with room cleanliness and maintenance. Guests have reported issues such as broken doors, non-functioning TVs, and occasional water discoloration. The staff is generally friendly, although some guests have expressed concerns about the quality of customer service and safety. Despite these challenges, the Super 8's affordability and location outside of Memphis' busier districts make it a practical option for short stays.

Nearby Attractions: Guests can explore the nearby attractions of Memphis, including the Memphis Zoo, Graceland, and Beale Street, all within a short driving distance from the motel.

122 | Tennessee Explorer's Bucket List

Tennessee Mountain Lodge

Location: 3571 Parkway, Pigeon Forge, TN 37863, United States
Plus code: QCPX+27 Pigeon Forge, Tennessee, USA
Contact: +1 323-300-5449
Website: www.oyorooms.com
Check-in time: 15:00
Check-out time: 11:00
Description: Tennessee Mountain Lodge offers an affordable stay with convenient access to Dollywood and other attractions in Pigeon Forge. The motel features a mix of modern and retro design elements, with some recently remodeled rooms and basic amenities. The property includes a clean and relaxing pool area. Rooms are equipped with essentials like a fridge and air conditioner, though some guests have noted varying cleanliness standards and occasional maintenance issues. The motel's location is a notable advantage for visitors exploring the local area.

Guests have reported that the lodge provides good value for its price, making it a suitable option for budget-conscious travelers. The motel's proximity to local activities and its straightforward, no-frills approach are appreciated by those seeking a practical place to stay. However, some have experienced issues such as unpleasant odors, minor maintenance problems, and occasional pest concerns. The Tennessee Mountain Lodge is an economical choice for those prioritizing location and cost over luxury.

Nearby Attractions: The motel is less than ten minutes from Dollywood and is conveniently located for exploring Pigeon Forge's attractions.

Mountain Vista Inn & Suites

Location: 2647 Parkway, Pigeon Forge, TN 37863, United States
Plus code: RC3G+J5 Pigeon Forge, Tennessee, USA
Contact: +1 865-365-4031
Website: www.mountainvistainn.com
Check-in time: 16:00
Check-out time: 11:00

Description: Mountain Vista Inn & Suites is ideally situated in Pigeon Forge, offering convenient access to local attractions such as Dollywood and various entertainment options. The property features spacious rooms, including some with two separate bedrooms connected by a vanity room and private bathroom. Although currently undergoing renovations, guests have praised the hotel's location and value for money. Rooms are described as clean and spacious, though some have noted issues such as inadequate air conditioning in certain rooms. The hotel includes a pool open until midnight, but does not provide pool towels, which must be requested from the front desk.

The hotel's proximity to the Island and other local attractions is a significant benefit, making it a good choice for those looking to explore Pigeon Forge. However, some guests have reported problems with pests and maintenance issues, suggesting that attention to these matters would enhance the overall guest experience. Despite these concerns, the Mountain Vista Inn & Suites remains a solid option for travelers seeking affordability and a central location.

Nearby Attractions: The hotel is within walking distance of various local attractions including go-karts, carnival rides, laser tag, virtual reality experiences, putt-putt golf, and the Ferris wheel.

Red Roof Inn Knoxville Central - Papermill Road

Location: 1315 Kirby Rd, Knoxville, TN 37909, United States

Plus code: WXWX+CW Knoxville, Tennessee, USA

Contact: +1 865-584-3911

Website: www.redroof.com

Check-in time: 14:00

Check-out time: 11:00

Description: The Red Roof Inn Knoxville Central - Papermill Road offers a budget-friendly option with a location that is convenient for travelers. The hotel features straightforward accommodations with basic amenities. While the location is considered decent, some guests have reported concerns about the facility's cleanliness and safety, with issues such as fingerprint dust on doors and unpleasant odors in the hallways. However, the service from the staff, particularly from a clerk named Jeff, has been noted as a highlight, providing helpful and accommodating assistance. The hotel rooms include king-size beds and are generally described as clean and comfortable, although some guests have mentioned problems with noisy air conditioning units and the lack of certain toiletries.

Nearby Attractions: The hotel is located within easy reach of various local dining options and shopping areas.

Restaurants

Monell's

Location: 1235 6th Ave N, Nashville, TN 37208, United States
Plus Code: 56G5+8V Nashville, Tennessee, USA
Contact: +1 615-248-4747
Website: www.monellstn.com
Opening Hours:
- Monday to Friday: 11am – 2:30pm, 5pm – 8:30pm
- Closed on Saturdays and Sundays

Description: Monell's in Nashville offers a true Southern dining experience with a focus on authentic, home-cooked meals. The restaurant features a family-style setup where large bowls of mashed potatoes, fried chicken, beans, and coleslaw are passed around at long tables, encouraging social interaction with fellow diners. The atmosphere is warm and welcoming, perfect for those ready to enjoy generous portions of comfort food. Meals are priced between $10 to $20 per person, providing a reasonable and hearty dining option. Check their website for daily changing entrees and additional menu options.
Nearby Attractions: Situated in the Germantown section, Monell's is close to various Nashville landmarks, including the Nashville Farmers' Market and the historic Germantown area.

The Loveless Cafe

Location: 8400 TN-100, Nashville, TN 37221, United States
Plus Code: 22PH+45 Nashville, Tennessee, USA
Contact: +1 615-646-9700
Website: www.lovelesscafe.com
Opening Hours:

- Monday to Saturday: 7am – 8pm
- Sunday: 7am – 3pm

Description: The Loveless Cafe offers a quintessential Southern dining experience known for its hearty breakfast and comforting meals. The cafe's signature homemade biscuits and preserves are a must-try, setting the tone for a meal featuring well-stuffed omelets, crisp waffles, and a variety of traditional dishes. The restaurant is renowned for its warm, cozy atmosphere and friendly service, making it a popular choice for breakfast and brunch. Expect to pay between $10 to $30 per person. Due to its popularity, reservations are recommended, especially on weekends when wait times can be longer. The walls are adorned with a collection of autographed photos, adding to the cafe's charm.

Nearby Attractions: Located in the scenic area of Nashville, The Loveless Cafe is close to the beautiful Radnor Lake State Park and the historic Belle Meade Plantation, making it a great spot for a meal before or after exploring these local landmarks.

Skull's Rainbow Room

Location: 222 Printers Alley, Nashville, TN 37219, United States
Plus Code: 567C+RF Nashville, Tennessee, USA
Contact: +1 615-810-9631
Website: www.skullsrainbowroom.com
Opening Hours:
- Monday to Friday: 5pm – 2am
- Saturday: 5pm – 2am
- Sunday: 10am – 2pm, 5pm – 2am

Description: Skull's Rainbow Room offers a unique blend of historic charm and modern elegance in the heart of Nashville's Printers Alley. Known for its vibrant atmosphere and live jazz performances, the venue creates an ideal setting for a memorable night out. The menu features a range of upscale dishes, including prime rib, New York strip, and specialty appetizers like lobster bisque soup and tuna tartare. Expect to spend between $50 to $100 per person. The restaurant's interior combines old-world sophistication with a lively, entertainment-focused environment. Reservations are recommended, especially during peak times, to ensure a prompt seating.

Nearby Attractions: Located in the historic Printers Alley, Skull's Rainbow Room is close to several notable Nashville landmarks, including the Ryman Auditorium and the Johnny Cash Museum, making it a great spot for dining before or after exploring these iconic sites.

Log Cabin Restaurant

Location: 15530 TN-13, Hurricane Mills, TN 37078, United States
Plus Code: V6J2+V7 Hurricane Mills, Tennessee, USA
Contact: +1 931-296-5311
Website: www.logcabinhmtn.com
Opening Hours:
- Monday to Sunday: 10:30am – 9pm

Description: Log Cabin Restaurant provides a classic Southern dining experience with generous portions and a welcoming atmosphere. The menu features hearty comfort foods such as roast beef, fried catfish, meatloaf, and a variety of sides like mashed potatoes, fried okra, and sweet potato casserole. Desserts, including chocolate meringue pie and pecan pie, are a highlight. With prices ranging from $10 to $20 per person, it offers a satisfying and affordable meal option. The restaurant is known for its friendly service and clean environment, making it a great stop for a home-cooked meal while traveling.

Nearby Attractions: Located in Hurricane Mills, the Log Cabin Restaurant is conveniently situated near attractions such as the Loretta Lynn's Ranch and the Tennessee River, offering visitors a chance to explore local sites before or after their meal.

Darfons Restaurant + Bar

Location: 2810 Elm Hill Pike, Nashville, TN 37214, United States
Plus Code: 48XP+G2 Nashville, Tennessee, USA
Contact: +1 615-889-3032
Website:
www.darfonsrestaurant.com
Opening Hours:
- Monday to Sunday: 11am – 9:30pm

Description: Darfons Restaurant + Bar is a standout dining spot in Nashville, known for its flavorful dishes and inviting atmosphere. The menu includes highlights such as barbecue-seared salmon, New Zealand lamb chops, and fried mozzarella cheese sticks. Desserts like key lime pie add a sweet finish to the meal. Prices range from $20 to $30 per person. The restaurant offers a cozy setting with attentive service, though parking can be limited during busy times. A parking lot is available with overflow options nearby.

Nearby Attractions: Darfons is conveniently located near attractions such as the Nashville Zoo and Percy Priest Lake, providing a great dining option before or after exploring these local sites.

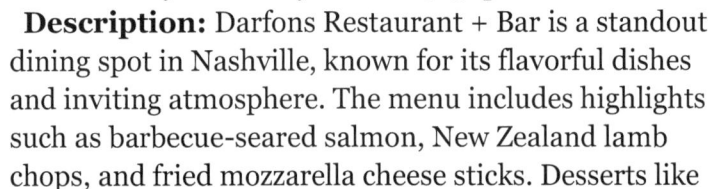

Feed Table and Tavern

Location: 201 W Main St, Chattanooga, TN 37402, United States
Plus Code: 2MPR+R5 Chattanooga, Tennessee, USA
Contact: +1 423-708-8500
Website:
www.feedtableandtavern.com

129 | Tennessee Explorer's Bucket List

Opening Hours:
- Monday to Sunday: 11am – 11pm

Description: Feed Table and Tavern offers a vibrant dining experience in Chattanooga with a menu featuring standout dishes like ribs, smoked wings, steak, and fried catfish. The atmosphere is casual yet stylish, making it a great spot for both lunch and dinner. The restaurant provides attentive service and a welcoming environment. Prices range from $10 to $50 per person. There is ample parking available, although it is paid street parking.

Nearby Attractions: Located in downtown Chattanooga, the restaurant is close to attractions like the Tennessee Aquarium and Lookout Mountain, ideal for dining before or after exploring these sites.

The Row Kitchen & Pub

Location: 110 Lyle Ave, Nashville, TN 37203, United States

Plus Code: 5622+GW Nashville, Tennessee, USA

Contact: +1 629-263-7418

Website: www.therownashville.com

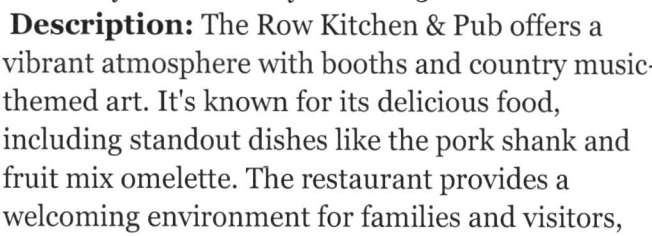

Opening Hours:
- Sunday to Thursday: 11am – 1am
- Friday and Saturday: 11am – 3am

Description: The Row Kitchen & Pub offers a vibrant atmosphere with booths and country music-themed art. It's known for its delicious food, including standout dishes like the pork shank and fruit mix omelette. The restaurant provides a welcoming environment for families and visitors, though service can be slow during busy times. Prices range from $10 to $50 per person. The location is central, making it a convenient choice for dining before or after exploring Nashville.

Nearby Attractions: Situated near downtown Nashville, The Row is close to music venues and other attractions like the Country Music Hall of Fame and Museum, ideal for a meal after enjoying local music and culture.

Jeff Ruby's Steakhouse, Nashville

Location: 300 4th Ave N, Nashville, TN 37219, United States
Plus Code: 568C+46 Nashville, Tennessee, USA
Contact: +1 615-434-4300
Website:
www.jeffruby.com

Opening Hours:
- Saturday: 4:30pm – 11pm
- Sunday: 4:30pm – 9pm
- Monday to Wednesday: 5pm – 10pm
- Thursday to Friday: 4:30pm – 11pm

Description: Jeff Ruby's Steakhouse in Nashville is renowned for its luxurious dining experience. The restaurant features an elegant ambiance with live piano music, a stylish interior, and impeccable service. Specialties include the Seafood Tower, Steak Collinsworth, and Jeff Ruby's Baked Macaroni & Cheese. The menu also offers a range of high-quality steaks and fresh seafood. Desserts like the skillet cookie and carrot cake are popular choices. Valet parking is available, and guests should expect a high-end dining experience with prices starting at $100 per person.

Nearby Attractions: Located in downtown Nashville, the steakhouse is close to attractions such as the Ryman Auditorium and Broadway's entertainment district.

High Point Restaurant

Location: 224 Main St, Monteagle, TN 37356, United States
Plus Code: 65QC+PG Monteagle, Tennessee, USA
Contact: +1 931-924-4600
Website: highpointrestaurant.net
Opening Hours:
- **Saturday:** 4–10 pm
- **Sunday:** 5–9 pm
- **Monday to Thursday:** 5–9 pm
- **Friday:** 5–10 pm

Description: High Point Restaurant offers a distinguished dining experience in Monteagle, known for its generous portions and exquisite desserts. Patrons rave about the Idaho Baked Potato and Bananas Foster, while the Lobster Bisque with Pastry Crouton and a Hint of Sherry and Grilled Pound Cake are also popular choices. The ambiance is complemented by exceptional service, with staff providing knowledgeable recommendations. Despite the higher price range, the quality of food and unique atmosphere make it a prime spot for special occasions.
Nearby Attractions: Located in a charming area with potential for exploring local historic sites and natural beauty.

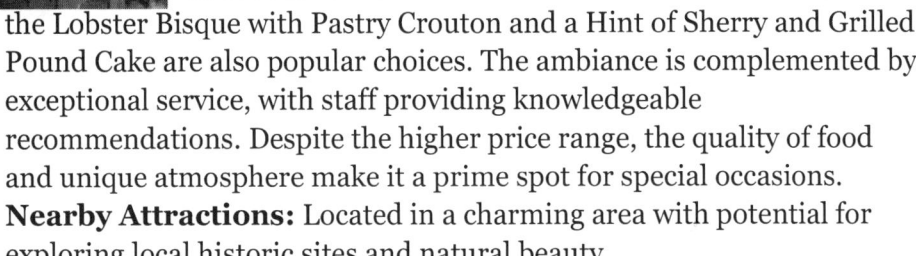

The 404 Kitchen

Location: 507 12th Ave S Fl 2, Nashville, TN 37203, United States
Plus Code: 5628+P4 Nashville, Tennessee, USA
Contact: +1 615-251-1404

Website: the404nashville.com

Opening Hours:
- **Monday to Thursday:** 5–10 pm
- **Friday to Saturday:** 5–11 pm
- **Sunday:** 5–9 pm

Description: The 404 Kitchen offers an exceptional dining experience in Nashville with a focus on flavorful dishes and a vibrant atmosphere. Guests appreciate the fresh and tasty cocktails, as well as the quality of the food, including standout items like trout, cornbread, and duck. The service, provided by knowledgeable and friendly staff, adds to the overall enjoyment. The restaurant also features a pleasant patio for dining during warmer months. Although some dishes like the twice-baked potatoes might be too spicy for certain palates, the majority of the experience is highly praised.

Nearby Attractions: Situated in a lively area of Nashville, the restaurant is close to various local attractions and entertainment options.

Bell Buckle Cafe

Location: 16 Railroad Sq TN-269, Bell Buckle, TN 37020, United States
Plus Code: HJQW+V3 Bell Buckle, Tennessee, USA
Contact: +1 931-389-9693
Website: ubereats.com

Opening Hours:
- **Monday to Saturday:** 11 am – 8 pm
- **Sunday:** Closed

Description: Bell Buckle Cafe is a beloved spot in Bell Buckle known for its flavorful Southern comfort food and welcoming atmosphere. The menu features standout items like the juicy pulled pork platter, homemade oatmeal cake, and peach cobbler. Other popular dishes include meatloaf, pork chops, and various sides such as turnip greens and carrot soufflé. The cafe is well-regarded for its friendly service and charming setting. Reservations are recommended due to frequent wait times, especially during peak hours.

Nearby Attractions: Located in a quaint area, the cafe is close to local shops and attractions, making it a great spot to visit while exploring Bell Buckle.

Where to get souvenir
Nashville Gifts

Location: 325 Broadway, Nashville, TN 37201, United States
Plus Code: 566F+98 Nashville, Tennessee, USA
Contact: +1 615-313-9926
Open Time:
- Saturday: 9 am–12 am
- Sunday: 9 am–11 pm
- Monday: 9 am–12 am
- Tuesday: 9 am–12 am
- Wednesday: 9 am–12 am
- Thursday: 9 am–12 am
- Friday: 9 am–12 am

Description: Nashville Gifts offers a diverse selection of souvenirs that include Nashville-themed items and classic keepsakes. The store is situated on Honky Tonk Highway, making it a convenient stop for visitors. It features a well-organized layout that makes browsing easy. The staff are noted for being helpful and can offer recommendations if needed. Prices vary, with items like crew neck sweatshirts priced around $50. This shop is an excellent choice for picking up memorable gifts and souvenirs from your Nashville visit.

Made in TN

Location: 3820 Charlotte Ave #127, Nashville, TN 37209, United States
Plus Code: 5539+55 Nashville, Tennessee, USA
Contact: +1 615-419-7761
Website: www.shopmadeintn.com
Open Time: 10 am–6 pm Daily

Description: Made in TN, located on the first floor of L & L Market, offers a variety of unique gifts and souvenirs that showcase local Tennessee products. The store features an array of gift baskets filled with specialty items, making it a great place to find distinctive presents for any occasion. The shop is women-owned and is known for its charming selection and personalized service. Prices vary based on the gift baskets, which cater to different budgets. The store's convenient location and thoughtful product selection make it an excellent stop for memorable Tennessee-themed gifts.

Legends Gifts

Location: 424 Broadway, Nashville, TN 37203, United States
Plus Code: 566C+8J Nashville, Tennessee, USA
Contact: +1 615-248-9264
Open Time:
- Saturday: 9 am–11 pm
- Sunday: 9 am–11 pm
- Monday: 9 am–11 pm
- Tuesday: 9 am–11 pm
- Wednesday: 9 am–11 pm
- Thursday: 9 am–11 pm
- Friday: 9 am–11 pm

Description: Legends Gifts is conveniently located on Broadway, right in the heart of Nashville's Honky Tonk Highway. This souvenir shop offers a wide range of items including clothing, magnets, spices, and ornaments. The store features a variety of T-shirts, often with unique designs like the "ITS ON THE BACK" tees. It also has a penny smashing machine and an Elvis Zoltar for a quirky touch. Prices vary, with T-shirts ranging from $16.99 to $30 and hoodies priced higher. The store is busy throughout the day and provides a good selection for visitors looking for Nashville-themed memorabilia.

The Nashville Store

Location: 433 Opry Mills Dr, Nashville, TN 37214, United States
Plus Code: 6825+73 Nashville, Tennessee, USA
Contact: +1 615-410-6686
Website:
www.thenashvillestore.com
Open Time:
- Saturday: 10 am–8 pm
- Sunday: 11 am–6 pm
- Monday: 10 am–8 pm
- Tuesday: 10 am–8 pm
- Wednesday: 10 am–8 pm
- Thursday: 10 am–8 pm
- Friday: 10 am–8 pm

Description: The Nashville Store, located in Opry Mills, offers a variety of Nashville-themed souvenirs, including trinkets and clothing. It provides a convenient option for last-minute gifts or keepsakes from Music City. The store features standard Nashville items, though some visitors might find the selection similar to other souvenir shops, with many products displaying similar designs. While the store is described as having friendly staff and being a decent stop for souvenirs, the quality and uniqueness of the items may not stand out compared to other local shops. Prices can be slightly high, but it may be a good option for those looking to avoid the more crowded areas on Broadway.

Made in TN

Location: 900 Rosa L Parks Blvd #125, Nashville, TN 37208, United States
Plus Code: 56C6+6F Nashville, Tennessee, USA
Contact: +1 615-717-2174
Website:
www.shopmadeintn.com

Open Time:
- Saturday: 8 am–6 pm
- Sunday: 9 am–5 pm
- Monday: 9 am–5 pm
- Tuesday: 9 am–5 pm
- Wednesday: 9 am–5 pm
- Thursday: 9 am–5 pm
- Friday: 9 am–5 pm

Description: Located within the Nashville Farmers' Market, Made in TN offers a wide range of reasonably priced souvenirs and local products. The store features a variety of items, including snacks made in Tennessee, such as GooGoo Clusters. It is a popular choice for visitors looking for affordable gifts and keepsakes. The shop is praised for its excellent service and ability to create personalized gift boxes for various occasions. With a focus on local goods and a commitment to quality, this store is a reliable option for unique and thoughtful gifts from Nashville.

Market Street Mercantile

Location: 111 2nd Ave N, Nashville, TN 37201, United States
Plus Code: 566F+VP Nashville, Tennessee, USA

Contact: +1 615-251-4092
Open Time:
- Saturday: 10 am–10 pm
- Sunday: 10 am–10 pm
- Monday: 10 am–10 pm
- Tuesday: 10 am–10 pm
- Wednesday: 10 am–10 pm
- Thursday: 10 am–10 pm
- Friday: 10 am–10 pm

Description: Market Street Mercantile is a charming shop in downtown Nashville offering a variety of souvenirs and gifts. The store features a well-curated selection of T-shirts and other memorabilia at reasonable prices. It is known for its friendly staff and exceptional customer service, with past visitors praising the helpfulness and kindness of the employees. The store is a great spot to pick up Nashville-themed items, whether for yourself or as gifts. The shop's location and extensive inventory make it a convenient and enjoyable place to find unique souvenirs.

Willie Nelson and Friends Museum and Nashville Souvenirs

Location: 2613A McGavock Pk, Nashville, TN 37214, United States
Plus Code: 6892+2P Nashville, Tennessee, USA
Contact: +1 615-885-1515
Website:
www.willienelsonmuseum.com
Open Time:
- Saturday: 9 am–8 pm
- Sunday: 9 am–8 pm
- Monday: 9 am–8 pm
- Tuesday: 9 am–8 pm
- Wednesday: 9 am–8 pm
- Thursday: 9 am–8 pm
- Friday: 9 am–8 pm

Description: Located in Music Valley Village, Willie Nelson and Friends Museum and Nashville Souvenirs offers a diverse range of memorabilia related to Willie Nelson and other music icons. The museum features various collectibles, including Willie Nelson merchandise, Elvis Presley items, hats, and unique souvenirs like the famous claw back scratcher. Visitors can also explore Nashville-themed souvenirs and treats, such as Goo Goo Bars. The museum provides a fun experience for music fans with opportunities to see live music nearby and enjoy friendly service. Although it primarily serves as a souvenir shop, the museum aspect and themed items make it a worthwhile stop for fans and souvenir hunters alike.

The Opry Shop

Location: 2804 Opryland Dr, Nashville, TN 37214, United States
Plus Code: 6844+QW
Nashville, Tennessee, USA
Website: www.store.opry.com
Open Time:
- Saturday: 10 am–9:30 pm
- Sunday: 10 am–4:30 pm
- Monday: 10 am–4:30 pm
- Tuesday: 10 am–4:30 pm
- Wednesday: 10 am–4:30 pm
- Thursday: 10 am–4:30 pm
- Friday: 10 am–9:30 pm

Description: Situated within the Grand Ole Opry grounds, The Opry Shop offers a wide range of memorabilia and souvenirs related to the iconic venue. The shop features a selection of Opry-branded goods, including high-quality T-shirts, hats, and posters. Visitors can find fun ornaments and a variety of other keepsakes. The shop is known for its affordable options and is a great place to pick up a memento of your visit. The Grand Ole Opry grounds provide ample free parking, although tours of the building require an additional fee. The

Opry Shop is a convenient stop for guests who want to remember their visit to one of country music's most famous landmarks.

Gift Horse

Location: 1006 Fatherland St #301, Nashville, TN 37206, United States
Plus Code: 56FX+JM Nashville, Tennessee, USA

Website: www.gifthorsenashville.com
Contact: +1 615-727-4404
Open Time:
- Saturday: 10:30 am–6 pm
- Sunday: 12–5 pm
- Monday: 12–6 pm
- Tuesday: 12–6 pm
- Wednesday: 10:30 am–6 pm
- Thursday: 10:30 am–6 pm
- Friday: 10:30 am–6 pm

Description: Located in the Fatherland District, Gift Horse is a charming shop known for its unique and carefully curated selection of gifts. The store offers a range of items, including cards, trinkets, jewelry, and vintage stationery. Gift Horse is recognized for its high-quality products and support of local artisans, making it a standout destination for finding special gifts and celebrating Nashville's vibrant community. The store is LGBTQ+ friendly and provides a welcoming shopping experience with friendly and helpful staff. Although prices may be slightly higher, the quality and uniqueness of the items make it worth a visit.

3-DAY ITINERARY

Day 1: Explore Nashville's Music History

Morning

1. **Country Music Hall of Fame and Museum**
   - **Description**: Discover the evolution of country music through interactive exhibits, iconic artifacts, and memorabilia from legendary stars. The museum also features a unique experience where you can record your own music.
   - **Cost**: Adults $27.95, Youth (6-12) $17.95, Under 6 Free
   - **Time Spent**: 2-3 hours
   - **Distance**: Located in downtown Nashville
2. **Ryman Auditorium**
   - **Description**: Visit the historic Ryman Auditorium, the original home of the Grand Ole Opry, and one of the most famous venues in music history. Take a backstage tour to learn about its impact on the country music scene.
   - **Cost**: Self-Guided Tour $26.95, Guided Backstage Tour $32.95
   - **Time Spent**: 1-2 hours
   - **Distance**: 0.4 miles (2-minute drive from Country Music Hall of Fame)

Afternoon

3. **Honky Tonk Highway (Broadway)**
   - **Description**: Enjoy live music along Nashville's famous Broadway strip, filled with honky tonk bars like Tootsie's Orchid Lounge and The Stage. Stroll and listen to performances throughout the day.

- **Cost**: Free to explore, drinks vary
- **Time Spent**: 1-2 hours
- **Distance**: Walking distance from Ryman Auditorium

4. **The Parthenon at Centennial Park**
   - **Description**: A full-scale replica of the Parthenon in Athens, this iconic landmark houses an art museum and features a 42-foot statue of Athena. The surrounding park is a great spot for a relaxing walk.
   - **Cost**: Adults $10, Children (4-17) $8
   - **Time Spent**: 1-2 hours
   - **Distance**: 2.3 miles (8-minute drive from Broadway)

Evening

5. **Grand Ole Opry**
   - **Description**: Cap off your day with a live show at the world-famous Grand Ole Opry, showcasing a mix of country legends and rising stars.
   - **Cost**: Ticket prices range from $45-$150
   - **Time Spent**: 2-3 hours
   - **Distance**: 12 miles (20-minute drive from Centennial Park)

Day 2: Pigeon Forge and Dollywood

Morning

1. **Dollywood (Pigeon Forge)**
   - **Description**: Dolly Parton's beloved theme park offers a blend of thrilling rides, live entertainment, and Southern crafts. It's fun for the whole family with roller coasters, shows, and delicious food options.
   - **Cost**: Adults $89, Children (4-9) $79

- Time Spent: 4-5 hours
- Distance: 213 miles from Nashville (3 hours 45 minutes)

Afternoon

2. **Titanic Museum Attraction**
   - **Description**: Explore the tragic voyage of the Titanic at this interactive museum, featuring more than 400 artifacts. You'll get a boarding pass and learn about the real-life passengers' stories.
   - **Cost**: Adults $35, Children (5-12) $15
   - **Time Spent**: 2-3 hours
   - **Distance**: 7.2 miles (15-minute drive from Dollywood)

Evening

3. **The Island in Pigeon Forge**
   - **Description**: This entertainment complex offers a variety of attractions, including The Great Smoky Mountain Wheel, live music, shops, and restaurants. A great spot for evening fun.
   - **Cost**: Free to explore, attraction costs vary
   - **Time Spent**: 2-3 hours
   - **Distance**: 6 miles (12-minute drive from Titanic Museum)

Day 3: Discover the Great Smoky Mountains

Morning

1. **Great Smoky Mountains National Park**
   - **Description**: A UNESCO World Heritage site, the Great Smoky Mountains offer breathtaking views, hiking trails, and wildlife. Start your day with a

scenic drive or a hike along trails like Laurel Falls or Alum Cave.
- **Cost**: Free
- **Time Spent**: 3-4 hours
- **Distance**: 15 miles from Pigeon Forge (30-minute drive)

2. **Clingmans Dome**
   - **Description**: Drive to the highest point in the Smoky Mountains, Clingmans Dome, and take the short hike to the observation tower for stunning panoramic views.
   - **Cost**: Free
   - **Time Spent**: 1-2 hours
   - **Distance**: 23 miles (1-hour drive from Pigeon Forge)

Afternoon

3. **Cades Cove**
   - **Description**: A beautiful valley surrounded by mountains, Cades Cove is one of the most popular spots in the park for wildlife viewing. Drive the 11-mile loop, where you might spot black bears, deer, and wild turkeys.
   - **Cost**: Free
   - **Time Spent**: 2-3 hours
   - **Distance**: 33 miles (1-hour drive from Clingmans Dome)

Evening

4. **Gatlinburg SkyLift Park**
   - **Description**: Enjoy the SkyLift to the top of Crockett Mountain and cross the SkyBridge, the longest pedestrian suspension bridge in North America, offering amazing views of the Smokies.
   - **Cost**: Adults $36.95, Children (4-11) $24.95
   - **Time Spent**: 1-2 hours

- **Distance**: 27 miles (45-minute drive from Cades Cove)

- **Total Driving Distance**: Approximately 500-600 miles
- **Estimated Costs per Person**: $300-$500 (excluding food, accommodations, and personal expenses)

7-DAY ITINERARY

Day 1: Explore Nashville's Music Scene
Morning
1. **Country Music Hall of Fame and Museum**
    - **Description**: A must-see for country music fans, this museum chronicles the rich history of the genre through exhibits, recordings, and memorabilia from legendary artists.
    - **Cost**: Adults $27.95, Youth (6-12) $17.95, Under 6 Free
    - **Time Spent**: 2-3 hours
    - **Distance**: Located in downtown Nashville
2. **Ryman Auditorium**
    - **Description**: Known as the "Mother Church of Country Music," this historic venue has hosted some of the biggest names in music since 1892. Take a backstage tour to see where legends performed.
    - **Cost**: Self-Guided Tour $26.95, Guided Backstage Tour $32.95
    - **Time Spent**: 1-2 hours
    - **Distance**: 0.4 miles (2-minute drive from Country Music Hall of Fame)

Afternoon
3. **Honky Tonk Highway**
    - **Description**: Nashville's famous Broadway strip is home to iconic honky tonk bars with live music all day. Visit

spots like Tootsie's Orchid Lounge or The Stage for a truly Nashville experience.
- **Cost**: Free to explore, drinks vary
- **Time Spent**: 1-2 hours
- **Distance**: Walking distance from Ryman Auditorium

4. **The Parthenon at Centennial Park**
   - **Description**: A full-scale replica of the ancient Greek Parthenon, this structure includes a 42-foot statue of Athena and serves as Nashville's art museum, featuring rotating exhibits.
   - **Cost**: Adults $10, Children (4-17) $8
   - **Time Spent**: 1-2 hours
   - **Distance**: 2.3 miles (8-minute drive from Ryman Auditorium)

Evening

5. **Grand Ole Opry**
   - **Description**: The ultimate venue for country music, the Grand Ole Opry features performances from rising stars and country legends alike. Experience the heart of Nashville's music scene live.
   - **Cost**: Ticket prices range from $45-$150
   - **Time Spent**: 2-3 hours
   - **Distance**: 12 miles (20-minute drive from The Parthenon)

Day 2: Dive into Nashville's History & Outdoors
Morning

1. **Andrew Jackson's Hermitage**
   - **Description**: Explore the home of the seventh U.S. President, Andrew Jackson. The Hermitage offers an immersive glimpse into the life and times of Jackson, with guided tours of the mansion and grounds.
   - **Cost**: Adults $25, Children (5-12) $16
   - **Time Spent**: 2-3 hours
   - **Distance**: 12.5 miles (25-minute drive from downtown Nashville)

Afternoon
2. **Belle Meade Historic Site & Winery**
   - **Description**: Once a thriving plantation, Belle Meade is now a historic site with a focus on Tennessee history. Take a tour and sample wine made from the on-site winery.
   - **Cost**: Tour and Wine Tasting $28, Children (7-18) $20
   - **Time Spent**: 2-3 hours
   - **Distance**: 6.7 miles (15-minute drive from downtown Nashville)
3. **Bicentennial Capitol Mall State Park**
   - **Description**: This beautiful park offers a 19-acre memorial to Tennessee's history, featuring monuments, fountains, and stunning views of the Tennessee State Capitol.
   - **Cost**: Free
   - **Time Spent**: 1-2 hours
   - **Distance**: 3.3 miles (8-minute drive from Belle Meade)

Evening
4. **The Escape Game Nashville (Downtown)**
   - **Description**: Test your problem-solving skills in an interactive escape room adventure. Great for groups, this thrilling experience offers several themed rooms to choose from.
   - **Cost**: $39.99 per person
   - **Time Spent**: 1 hour
   - **Distance**: 3 miles (10-minute drive from Bicentennial Park)

Day 3: Experience Pigeon Forge and the Smoky Mountains
Morning
1. **Dollywood**
   - **Description**: Dolly Parton's famous theme park blends Southern charm with thrilling rides, live entertainment, and craft demonstrations. Great for families and anyone who loves fun and excitement.
   - **Cost**: Adults $89, Children (4-9) $79
   - **Time Spent**: 4-6 hours
   - **Distance**: 213 miles from Nashville (3 hours 45 minutes)

Afternoon
2. **Dolly's Tennessee Mountain Home**
    - **Description**: Visit the original childhood home of Dolly Parton, which is preserved as part of Dollywood. It's a great stop for Dolly fans to reflect on her humble beginnings.
    - **Cost**: Free (Part of Dollywood)
    - **Time Spent**: 30 minutes
    - **Distance**: Located within Dollywood
3. **Titanic Museum Attraction**
    - **Description**: Step into the shoes of a Titanic passenger at this interactive museum. Featuring over 400 artifacts from the ship, this museum provides an in-depth look at the ship's ill-fated voyage.
    - **Cost**: Adults $35, Children (5-12) $15
    - **Time Spent**: 2-3 hours
    - **Distance**: 7.2 miles (15-minute drive from Dollywood)

Evening
4. **Great Smoky Mountains National Park**
    - **Description**: This UNESCO World Heritage site is renowned for its natural beauty and diverse wildlife. Explore scenic drives, easy hikes, or enjoy breathtaking views from Clingmans Dome.
    - **Cost**: Free
    - **Time Spent**: 2-3 hours (Optional sunset hike or drive)
    - **Distance**: 20 miles (40-minute drive from Pigeon Forge)

Day 4: Knoxville and Scenic Drives
Morning
1. **Knoxville's Rowing Man Statue**
    - **Description**: A famous public sculpture, the Rowing Man Statue is a symbol of the city's sports culture and connection to the nearby Tennessee River.
    - **Cost**: Free
    - **Time Spent**: 30 minutes
    - **Distance**: 20 miles from the Great Smoky Mountains (45-minute drive)

Afternoon
2. **Tennessee Aquarium (Chattanooga)**
   - **Description**: Home to one of the world's largest freshwater exhibits, this aquarium offers stunning views of marine life, from river otters to sharks.
   - **Cost**: Adults $39.95, Children (3-12) $29.95
   - **Time Spent**: 2-3 hours
   - **Distance**: 110 miles from Knoxville (1 hour 45-minute drive)

Evening
3. **Rock Island State Park**
   - **Description**: A beautiful park featuring waterfalls, rugged hiking trails, and opportunities for swimming and boating. It's a great way to experience Tennessee's natural beauty.
   - **Cost**: Free
   - **Time Spent**: 2-3 hours
   - **Distance**: 95 miles from Chattanooga (1 hour 45-minute drive)

Day 5: Historic Homes and Natural Wonders
Morning
1. **Carnton Plantation**
   - **Description**: A key site in the Battle of Franklin, this historic home offers guided tours that cover the Civil War and its impact on Tennessee.
   - **Cost**: Adults $18, Children (6-12) $10
   - **Time Spent**: 2-3 hours
   - **Distance**: 113 miles from Rock Island (2-hour drive)

Afternoon
2. **Natchez Trace Parkway Bridge**
   - **Description**: One of the most scenic drives in the United States, the Natchez Trace Parkway offers stunning views, with the iconic double-arch bridge being a highlight.
   - **Cost**: Free
   - **Time Spent**: 1-2 hours
   - **Distance**: 25 miles from Franklin (30-minute drive)

Evening
3. **Leiper's Fork**
    - **Description**: A charming village with art galleries, boutique shops, and restaurants. It's a great place to unwind and experience small-town Tennessee.
    - **Cost**: Free to explore
    - **Time Spent**: 2-3 hours
    - **Distance**: 6 miles from Natchez Trace (10-minute drive)

Day 6: Adventure and Art
Morning
1. **Cumberland Caverns**
    - **Description**: One of the longest caves in the U.S., offering tours of beautiful underground formations and adventurous cave experiences like spelunking.
    - **Cost**: Adults $29.95, Children (6-12) $19.95
    - **Time Spent**: 2-3 hours
    - **Distance**: 57 miles from Franklin (1 hour 15-minute drive)

Afternoon
2. **Chattanooga's Hunter Museum of American Art**
    - **Description**: This museum features a collection of American art ranging from the Colonial period to the modern day, all housed in a striking contemporary building.
    - **Cost**: Adults $20, Children (3-17) $10
    - **Time Spent**: 1-2 hours
    - **Distance**: 87 miles from Cumberland Caverns (1 hour 45-minute drive)

Evening
3. **Tennessee Riverwalk**
    - **Description**: A scenic 13-mile paved trail along the Tennessee River, perfect for walking, biking, or enjoying views of the water and surrounding cityscape.
    - **Cost**: Free
    - **Time Spent**: 1-2 hours
    - **Distance**: 5 miles from Hunter Museum (10-minute drive)

Day 7: Memphis and Civil Rights History

Morning

1. **Graceland**
   - **Description**: The home of Elvis Presley, Graceland offers an inside look at the King of Rock 'n' Roll's life, including his famous Jungle Room, car collection, and final resting place.
   - **Cost**: Tour packages range from $48-$77
   - **Time Spent**: 3-4 hours
   - **Distance**: 210 miles from Chattanooga (3 hours 15-minute drive)

Afternoon

2. **National Civil Rights Museum**
   - **Description**: Located at the Lorraine Motel, the site where Dr. Martin Luther King Jr. was assassinated, this museum offers an in-depth look at the history of the civil rights movement.
   - **Cost**: Adults $18, Children (5-17) $15
   - **Time Spent**: 2-3 hours
   - **Distance**: 8.5 miles from Graceland (15-minute drive)

Evening

3. **Beale Street**
   - **Description**: Famous for its vibrant nightlife, Beale Street is lined with live music venues, restaurants, and bars offering the best of Memphis blues and soul.
   - **Cost**: Free to explore, drinks and food vary
   - **Time Spent**: 2-3 hours
   - **Distance**: 1 mile from Civil Rights Museum (5-minute drive)

FUN AND FASCINATING FACTS ABOUT TENNESSEE

1. Did you know Tennessee is home to the most visited national park in the U.S.?
The Great Smoky Mountains National Park, which straddles the Tennessee-North Carolina border, attracts over 12 million visitors annually, making it the most visited national park in the country.

2. Did you know Tennessee is known as the "Volunteer State"?
The nickname originated during the War of 1812 when thousands of Tennessee volunteers, including frontiersman Davy Crockett, enlisted to fight, gaining a reputation for their courageous efforts.

3. Did you know the state capital, Nashville, is called "Music City"?
Nashville earned this nickname due to its rich history in the music industry, especially as the epicenter of country music. It's also home to the Grand Ole Opry and the Country Music Hall of Fame.

4. Did you know Tennessee was the birthplace of rock 'n' roll?
Memphis is where Elvis Presley, the "King of Rock 'n' Roll," recorded his first songs at Sun Studio. It's also home to Graceland, one of the most visited homes in America.

5. Did you know the world's largest underground lake is in Tennessee?
The Lost Sea in Sweetwater, Tennessee, is the largest underground lake in the U.S. and the second-largest in the world, offering boat tours on its clear waters.

6. Did you know Tennessee played a crucial role in the Civil Rights Movement?
The Lorraine Motel in Memphis is where Dr. Martin Luther King Jr. was assassinated in 1968. Today, it's the site of the National Civil Rights Museum, chronicling the fight for racial equality.

7. Did you know Tennessee is a major whiskey producer?
The state is known for its Tennessee whiskey, with Jack Daniel's being the most famous distillery. Located in Lynchburg, Jack Daniel's has been in operation since 1866.

8. Did you know the Tennessee River is the largest tributary of the Ohio River?

The Tennessee River spans 652 miles, winding through the state and offering scenic beauty, water sports, and fishing opportunities.

9. Did you know Tennessee is home to the first public park in the U.S.?
Shelby Farms Park in Memphis is one of the largest urban parks in the country, featuring over 4,500 acres of green space and outdoor activities.

10. Did you know the Oak Ridge National Laboratory played a key role in the Manhattan Project?
Oak Ridge, Tennessee, was a secret city during World War II, where scientists worked on the development of the atomic bomb as part of the Manhattan Project.

11. Did you know the famous Bristol Motor Speedway is in Tennessee?
One of NASCAR's most iconic tracks, Bristol Motor Speedway in Bristol, Tennessee, is known for its steep banking and is a favorite venue for racing fans.

12. Did you know Tennessee has more than 9,000 caves?
The state is famous for its extensive cave systems, including Cumberland Caverns and Ruby Falls, one of the tallest underground waterfalls in the U.S.

13. Did you know Tennessee was the last state to join the Confederacy and the first to rejoin the Union?
Tennessee seceded from the Union in 1861 but was the first Confederate state to be readmitted to the Union in 1866, following the Civil War.

14. Did you know Tennessee has three distinct regions?
The state is divided into East, Middle, and West Tennessee, each with its own unique geography, culture, and economy, from the mountains in the east to the fertile plains in the west.

15. Did you know the longest pedestrian suspension bridge in North America is in Tennessee?
Located in Gatlinburg, the SkyBridge stretches 680 feet across a deep valley and offers breathtaking views of the Great Smoky Mountains.

16. Did you know the infamous Scopes Monkey Trial took place in Tennessee?

In 1925, Dayton, Tennessee, was the site of the famous trial where teacher John Scopes was prosecuted for teaching evolution, sparking national debate over science and religion.

17. Did you know the Tennessee Walking Horse is world-renowned?
Tennessee is famous for the Tennessee Walking Horse, a breed known for its smooth gait and used in horse shows, competitions, and trail riding around the world.

18. Did you know the state song of Tennessee is "Rocky Top"?
Tennessee has multiple official state songs, but "Rocky Top," a bluegrass hit from the 1960s, is perhaps the most beloved and frequently played at University of Tennessee sporting events.

19. Did you know Dollywood is one of the top theme parks in the U.S.?
Located in Pigeon Forge, Dollywood, owned by country music icon Dolly Parton, attracts over 3 million visitors annually with its rides, music shows, and Appalachian-themed attractions.

20. Did you know Tennessee's Reelfoot Lake was created by an earthquake?
Reelfoot Lake, in the northwest corner of the state, was formed by the New Madrid earthquakes of 1811–1812, which caused the Mississippi River to temporarily flow backward, filling the lake.

TRAVEL

DATE:

DURATION:

DESTINATION:

PLACES TO SEE:

1. _____
2. _____
3. _____
4. _____
5. _____
6. _____
7. _____

LOCAL FOOD TO TRY:

1. _____
2. _____
3. _____
4. _____
5. _____
6. _____
7. _____

NOTES

EXPENSES IN TOTAL:

JOURNAL

TRAVEL

DATE:
DURATION:

DESTINATION:

PLACES TO SEE:	LOCAL FOOD TO TRY:
1	1
2	2
3	3
4	4
5	5
6	6
7	7

NOTES

EXPENSES IN TOTAL:

JOURNAL